BLUE-COLLAR MINISTRY

FACING ECONOMIC AND SOCIAL REALITIES OF WORKING PEOPLE

TEX SAMPLE

Judson Press® Valley Forge

BLUE COLLAR MINISTRY

Copyright © 1984
Judson Press, Valley Forge, PA 19482-0851
Second Printing, 1987

Library of Congress Cataloging in Publication Data

Sample, Tex.
    Blue collar ministry.
    Includes bibliographical references and index.
    1. Church work with laboring classes.   I. Title.
BV2695.W6S36 1984   261.8'34562'0973   84-3888
ISBN 0-8170-1029-7

Dedicated to:

A. C. Sample
Helen Sartin Sample
Irene D. Sanford

and in memory of:

T. G. Sanford

Preface

It is my conviction that the church does not understand working-class people, and that ministry with working-class people is not a priority for most main-line denominations. What follows in these pages, then, is an attempt to change this situation.

The focus of the book is decidedly local: the local community and the local church. Its primary audience will be pastors and other religious professionals who work—or want to work—with blue-collar people inside and outside the church. People working in related fields will also find the book to be helpful. With the exception of a discussion of community organizations and citizens organizations, however, labor unions and other secular agencies—as important as they are—will not be discussed. An abundance of literature on such organizations already exists.

The concern here is primarily with Protestant churches and with white, blue-collar Americans. I am aware that many working-class people are not Protestant but Catholic. Of these, many are white ethnics who live in the northeastern part of the United States, along the Atlantic seaboard and across the midwest industrial centers of Cleveland, Gary, Chicago and so on. These are also the working people who have received the most attention in social-science literature. While ethnic Catholics are not absent from this study, I have tried to give more attention to the white, Protestant, working-class people of our country and to the ways that main-line churches can respond to them.

The first step is to move beyond the stereotype so many church professionals have of blue-collar people. Chapter 1 describes this stereotype and suggests a definition of blue-collar people to be used throughout the study.

The next step requires an appreciation for the crunch blue-collar people experience, caught between the achievement values of the United States culture and the restricted opportunities of the working class. Part I discusses this crunch in terms of the religion of winning and the reality of losing.

The responses blue-collar people make to this contradiction of culture and opportunity are not all one kind. Working-class people are a diverse group, and Part II describes four basic lifestyles that have been reported in sociological research. Part II is the result of my concern to bring together for the church professional some of the best research on working-class people. One aspect of this book is thus reportorial.

What place do religion and the church have in the lives of the working class? The first chapter of Part III reports on the basic religious expressions of blue collarites: their denominational affiliation, church attendance, and so on. The next two chapters develop a response that the church can make and suggest a basic role for the pastor who serves working-class people in the church and in the community.

Part IV addresses the question of how blue collarites and churches at the local level can make an impact on systemic issues. New methods of community organization were developed in the 1970s and the early 1980s, and key ingredients in these methods are discussed. The last chapter proposes a role for the church in these new forms of community organization.

I have worked on this issue of the church and the blue-collar American for about fifteen years. During that length of time the list of people to whom I am indebted has grown too long to register here. I hope the book will be an expression of my gratitude to them.

Other persons, however, have made specific contributions too important not to mention.

I am indebted to Saint Paul School of Theology, its trustees, faculty, and administration for a generous sabbatical leave during the academic year of 1982–1983. William K. McElvaney, president, and E. Dale Dunlap, academic dean, have especially encouraged me in my work on this manuscript.

My gratitude goes particularly to Larry Don Hollon of the National Council of Churches. He and I have taught a course at Saint Paul on country music and the blue-collar American for a number of years. His influence throughout these pages is pervasive. I also want to thank the students who have taken the course. Their insight and clarification helped my understanding.

Several friends and colleagues have read parts or all of the manuscript. Had I been able to take better advantage of their suggestions, the book would have been stronger. I am, of course, responsible for the content, but without their help the weaknesses would have been even more evident. I want to thank Neil Blair, Evelyn Fisher, Kevin Lagree, Gene Lowry, William B. McClain, Richard Seaton, Susan Vogel, and Larry Wright.

Lydia Cantrill, a secretary at Saint Paul, worked devotedly through several typings of the manuscript. She was more than a typist, however, because her comments on the material—growing out of her own life—went well beyond her duties. She has my appreciation and respect.

I owe a deep debt to Snooks Britt, Bernell Birch, Jeep Pickett, and John Case who instructed me in the oil fields of Mississippi. Hart Field, Margaret Jones, and Phillip Nason trained me at the People's Methodist Church in Haverhill, Massachusetts.

Harold L. Twiss of Judson Press was a gentle but perceptive and careful editor of these pages. I needed and appreciated his thorough attention and professional guidance.

Finally, anyone who knows anything about my spouse, Peggy, knows how profoundly she has graced my life and my work.

Tex Sample

Contents

Introduction: Who Is the Blue-Collar American?

No we don't fit in with that white collar crowd
We're a little too rowdy and a little too loud
But there's no place that I'd rather be than right here
With my red neck, white socks and Blue Ribbon Beer.[1]

I was doing church development work in a small city—about 150,000 residents—with a significant population of working-class people. One day I rode with two pastors and a denominational executive down state highway 96 looking at subdivisions as potential sites for a new church.

We turned into one subdivision, and I saw a familiar scene: pickup trucks with gun racks in the rear windows, motorcycles parked in front yards, and oversized statuary that dominated well-kept lawns. In front of one house sat a '57 Chevrolet with its hood up and, beside it, the head of the engine resting on two concrete blocks. The houses had a subdivision sameness about them. They were nice but smaller and less expensive than houses in more affluent suburbs.

In my mind I walked in the front door of my childhood home and could feel the contoured, gold carpet of the living room beneath my feet. Plastic plants and flowers adorned the walls and the dining-room table at the far end of the living room. The TV set was the centerpiece of the room. On it and on the wall around it was a homey collection of family pictures: sons, daughters, parents, grandparents, uncles, aunts, nephews, nieces, cousins, and young people serving in the armed forces. Standing guard over flowers and pictures were two trophies from a bowling league, one dated 1969 and the other 1971.

"Well, I don't think we'll find many of our church members here. Let's move on down to the next subdivision." This comment jarred me from my reverie, and the driver made two left turns to put us back on the highway.

From a previous conversation I knew that the minister who made the comment had come from a blue-collar family. It was also clear that he had rejected those roots.

As we rode along, he and the other minister, both successful in their careers, began to talk.

"If those people go to church at all, they seem to want to go to conservative or fundamèntalist churches. They want somebody to tell them what to believe rather than to think for themselves."

"Yes," answered the minister from the working family, "but not many of them go to church anyhow, especially the men."

"And they just don't seem to be comfortable in our churches. Somehow we just don't seem to attract them."

Two subdivisions later we were in a place where the homes were worth over a hundred thousand dollars apiece.

"Now," said the other man, "this is where *our* church people are. We would find many fine members here."

I wondered what made the one man so estranged from his blue-collar origins. What made him talk about "they" and "them" when discussing the group of people from whom he came?

I knew that he had attended a fine theological school at which he developed an appreciation for the scholarly life and the world of ideas. His sermons were thoughtful and well delivered. He appreciated art and the finer things of life. While he socialized with important people around town, he cared about social issues. He had been courageous in the civil-rights struggle. His comments were informed by a well-above-average reading of black and liberation theology, and he had begun an effort to understand feminist thought. A lover of music, he collected records of spirituals and folk music and even liked a rarified form of blue grass. He had been raised on country music, but I discovered he could not now "stand the stuff."

I glanced at his conservative, three-piece, brown suit with a tasteful striped tie. I could not find a blue-collar thread in him, until later. That night in his basement he showed me his workshop.

"This is where I really live. When I'm down here working with my hands, the time flies."

"Where did you get your interest in woodworking?"

"From my dad. He was a factory worker. He could do anything with his hands. As a youngster, I marveled at what he could do with wood. Our house was small, but the basement was a workshop. It had the smell of different woods: walnut, oak, cedar. It was a great place to be. The smell and the feel of wood . . . ah!

"The folks never had much, but Dad gave me my interest in woodworking. I suppose I would have been a factory worker, too, but the folks wanted me to go to college. And here I am, sneaking off as often as I can to come down here."

"What about your mom?"

"Oh, she worked, too, besides at home. She was a production worker in a small plant—spent a good part of her life there. It seemed to take both their paychecks to make it. I saw enough to know that I wanted to go to school to get away from that kind of life."

As we talked in his workshop, I felt stalked by despair, by an awareness that was more emptying than threatening; I felt a loss of hope that the church could build an authentic relationship with working-class people. If this man—raised in a blue-collar family, sophisticated, sensitive to the issues of race and gender, and captivated by working with his hands—could not cross the dividing walls of class, then who could?

I went to the motel depressed. The day's events were not dramatic; there was nothing ominous. I thought how pervasive the barrier of class could be in everyday chance happenings. I was depressed about an able, sensitive human being not owning his roots, his background, his people, except in the basement of his home.

I also saw myself in that situation. My family had been working-class people, and I had spent almost fifteen years trying to be an intellectual and to escape.

My mother had awakened me every morning with country music loud on the radio and a warm kiss on the cheek. I liked the kiss; but I spent twenty-five years trying to hate the music. During World War II Mom was the *first* woman school-bus driver we had ever heard of in south Mississippi. My earliest memories of my dad were from the late thirties when he delivered blocks of ice early in the morning in an old truck he named "Asthma." After the ice deliveries, he drove a school bus and then worked most of the day as a shoe cobbler, breaking his afternoon by taking the schoolchildren back home on the bus. He then returned to the shoe shop and finished work at 6 P.M. or later.

I still remembered a kind of boundary between most of the working-class people I knew and the people who went to First Methodist Church. It was not nearly so castelike as the wall between blacks and whites, but it was very real.

I remembered, too, when I pastored a small church made up mostly of working-class people and decided to teach a church school class—sort of "the pastor's class." The first Sunday fifteen people showed, and I announced that we would be studying the philosophy of religion. The next Sunday there were five, and we abandoned the class on the fourth Sunday when one loyal soul remained.

I was depressed at the motel that night because I wondered if the church really could relate to working-class people. It seems that main-line churches have become increasingly middle class and "out of touch." Of course, there *are* working-class people in the churches, and there are blue-collar churches, but the main-line denominations seem to be increasingly middle class in orientation. A class barrier pervades churches, making an authentic relationship between the church and working-class people difficult, to say the least.

This barrier of class rests in part on a stereotype of blue-collar people, a caricature that puts distance between them and the middle class. In this stereotype blue-collar men are rednecks, bigots, racists, and fanatics and under their hardhats lies "the great American desert," as one writer has described it.[2] They work at jobs that pay too much, have too many benefits, and too much union protection. They drink too much, carouse too much, fight too much, and chase too many women. They wear cowboy boots on their feet and Caterpillar hats on their heads and their beer bellies hang out over big, buckled belts whose capacity to hold up sagging pants defies scientific understanding. They spend their lives working, watching sports on TV, and hanging out in honky-tonks.

In this stereotype blue-collar women are called basically "wives" or "the wife." They are caught up in the home, isolated from the world, and take care of a brood of kids. They wear the fashionable hairdos of five and ten years ago. If they are young and pretty, they are narcissistic and mindless. If they are older, they are brassy and have leathered skin that makes them look hard. Around the house their hair is in curlers, which provide the crown for a housecoat that looks cheap because it's too pretentious. They work in low-paying factory jobs where their mascara and polish on artificial nails are shrill incongruities with work aprons and the production line. The stereotype is pervasive.

I know intellectuals and liberals who maintain the highest ethical standards in their language about blacks, women, Asians, Native Americans, Hispanics, and other groups. Highly circumspect about avoiding racial, ethnic, and sexist slurs, they seem to think nothing of making the most degrading comments about working-class people. For every joke a bigot knows about blacks, such people know one about rednecks, who seem to be universally working class.

To be sure, if one has a stereotype about working-class people, one will find representatives to fit it, but contradictions to the stereotype will also be found. One can find people like Archie

Bunker, Edith, or Hollywood's "Joe" of some years ago, but these caricatures do so much definitional violence to blue-collar people that they constitute an outright falsification. What they portray is the stereotype America has of working-class people, embodying the class system so deeply writ, though usually unacknowledged, in our culture.

The stereotyping has plenty of intellectual and academic support as well. Aiming to please the college-age, counter-culture crowd he loved so much, Charles Reich referred to blue-collar workers in terms of ". . . their sullen boredom, their unchanging routines, their minds closed to new ideas and new feelings, their bodies slumped in front of television to watch the ballgame Sunday."[3] Or listen to Emile Pin, who ought to know better, as he wrote of the proletariat:

> Its members dispose of none of the means by which they might integrate themselves or find a recognized and stable place in urban society. They possess neither the financial reserves, nor the social connections, nor, *most important, the cultural level and the personal education which would permit them to master complex situations* and to separate the individual psychological life from the social life in which the individual is immersed. *Suspicion, adolescent aggressiveness, uncooperativeness are normal in men who live in and must make their living from a world which does not possess by itself an immediate and visible coherence.* Not only do they not understand this world, but further, they do not enjoy in it an equal share in the allotment of its most diverse advantages. *The proletariat is in the first place proletarian because of its lack of intellectual and social education, then because of all the other deprivations* suffered by its members, all of these deprivations being aggravated by the fundamental lack of adaptation [author's emphasis].[4]

Both Reich and Pin grant that social constraints operate against blue-collar people; yet the problem seems to be mainly in working-class heads. If these working-class people were more cultured, better educated, more open to expansive life-styles and new experiences, less adolescent and more cooperative, less stuck in their ways, and had a more "coherent" under-standing of the world, *then* they would be more adaptive and more human.

When one reads comments like these of Reich and Pin, Lillian

Rubin's point takes on a jarring significance: "portrayals of the flesh-and-blood people who make up America's working class—portrayals that tell us something of the texture and fabric of their lives, that deal respectfully with their manners, mores, and values—are notably few."[5] Understanding working-class people requires a deeper look than the easy generalizations of common opinion, the simplistic typologies of some social science, and the biases that dominate the response of the church and its leaders.

The stereotype of blue-collar people grows, in part, from their commitment to traditional values: family, faith, neighborhood, and country. In the stereotype these result in wrongheaded parochialism and superpatriotism. These traditional values—so the stereotype goes—root working-class members in concrete: they are unable and unwilling to move out of a status quo that renders their lives dull, deadened, and routinized. More than that, the stereotype views this commitment to traditional values as the reason for the susceptibility of blue-collar people to every demagogue, racist, and authoritarian figure that comes along.

It will be my contention that these traditional values require reexamination to determine whether they are cause for despair or for hope, whether they soak up energy into a status quo sump or propel working-class people toward new possibilities. Such a reexamination will seek to view these traditional values in the larger context of American culture and the situations blue-collar people face in their everyday lives. In order to turn to these, a working definition of the blue-collar American will be necessary.

In these pages working-class people will be defined by occupation: craft and kindred workers, operatives, laborers, and service workers. Obviously not all service workers should be included, but the typically low incomes of the people in this sector and the hard physical work most of them do are reasons for their inclusion. Secretaries and clerical workers will not be included. While some suggest that in America the office is a factory and that some secretarial pools and clerical operations are similar to production lines, the inclusion of these groups would cast the net too wide and would not focus as specifically on the group of Americans that I want to discuss most closely.

Even when constricting the definition of working-class people this much, we find much variation among them. In fact, perhaps the best generalization that can be made about blue-collar people is that they are diverse. No single image covers the flesh-and-blood reality of their lives. They are diverse by virtue of ethnicity, race, gender, generation, religion, and region of the country. The work they do for a living varies greatly as does its impact on their lives. The relationships that occur within the families change from household to household.

One of the most measurable instances of working-class diversity is in personal and family income. In 1980 the median income of a blue-collar man was $12,392. For blue-collar women the figure was $6,750. The median income of a service-sector man was $6,214; for a woman it was $3,004.

Most blue-collar and service-sector families are two-income families. The following table records the number and percent of families at different income levels. It should be remembered that these are incomes of families in which at least one householder was employed during 1980.

Family Incomes of Craft and Kindred Workers, Operatives, Laborers, and Service Workers, 1980[6]

Family Income	Number of Families (in thousands)	Percent of Total Number of Families
$0–$9,999	3,241	13.8
$10,000–$19,999	7,648	32.6
$20,000–$29,999	7,180	30.6
$30,000–$39,999	3,526	15.0
$40,000–$49,999	1,223	5.2
$50,000 +	633	2.6

From the table it is clear that 13.8 percent of blue-collar families with an employed householder made less than $10,000 for the year. Even by conservative government standards most of these families were poor.

Roughly one-third of the working-class families had incomes between $10,000 and $20,000. Many of these families could be considered near-poor.

Over 30 percent of the working-class families earned between $20,000 and $30,000. Most of these families had incomes that exceeded the median family income in the United States, which was $23,823 in 1980 for families with an employed householder.

Blue-collar aristocrats—as they are sometimes called—would be those families with more than $30,000 in income. They made up 22.8 percent of the working class. Those who made more than $40,000 constituted only 7.8 percent.

On the basis of these wide-ranging family incomes alone, one might expect great differences of life-style among working people. The expectation would be correct. Yet differences in life-style are related to a range of factors. The life-styles of blue-collar people are affected by their values, the power of the groups to which they belong, their work and life experience in everyday social encounters, and the opportunities available to them.

If the church is to have an effective ministry to and with working-class people, an understanding of and an appreciation for their life-styles and their diversity are essential. This involves looking at the conditions that shape their lives. There is no better way to begin that understanding than to look at American culture and the religion of winning.

Part I

The Religion of Winning and the Reality of Losing

1

The Religion of Winning

When I was fourteen, I answered the phone for the local Yellow Cab company of which my Dad was owner and operator. The outfit had four to seven cars depending on which year it was and the incessant amount of wreckage brought on by hiring drivers who were young and wild or older and full of drink. The parking lot behind the cabstand was sixty-three feet wide with Mr. Perkin's furniture store on one side and Almand's cleaners on the other. With Mr. Perkin's retroactive permission, I drew a strike zone on his store wall and scraped up gravel near the cleaners for a mound. I purchased three rubber-coated baseballs for forty-nine cents each, and I began to pelt that wall with the balls, trying to hit the strike zone—a pursuit that turned out to be the impossible dream.

One day my Uncle Paul, who owned the local fish market and later distinguished himself as the town's fire chief, walked up and asked me, "Boy, do you want to be a pitcher?"

"Worse than anything in the world."

"Well, there ain't but two things you gotta do. You gotta want to bad enough, and you gotta work hard enough."

"Is that really true, Uncle Paul?" I asked, because I really didn't know anyone who wanted to more than I did, and in all the years I played ball, I had never played on a team with anyone who worked harder than I did.

"Shore it's true. You can do anything you want to if you work hard enough and want to bad enough. Hell, look at Babe Ruth. If he could do it, you can."

This event is the most vivid memory I have of a major dimension of the American Dream: that effort and desire are the requisites of achievement, indeed of being Number One.

Subsequent events proved that my Uncle Paul was correct. I could have played major-league ball. I had everything it took, well, except for three things—three things that Babe Ruth could do and I couldn't: Ruth could run, and I couldn't; Ruth could throw, and I couldn't; Ruth could hit, and I couldn't. But except for those three things, I could have made it to the big leagues.

What weighed heavily on me, however, was the feeling that somehow I was to blame, that finally it was my fault because the desire and the effort had fallen short. I still catch myself on occasion fantasizing, *If I had known about weight-training in those days or if I had gripped my fast ball* with *the seams instead of* across *them or if I had had good coaching or if. . . .* But the truth of the matter is that no amount of effort and desire could have overcome my sheer lack of talent. Someone might attempt to console me by suggesting that there are physical limitations and that hard work and effort cannot overcome some things. I, of course, *have* to agree.

Something in the American psyche will allow certain *physical* limitations but is enormously resistant to the notion that there are *social* limitations that are structural, that these are more powerful than physical or mental limitations, and that they are not typically overcome by great desire and hard work. The reasons for this are religious. By "religious" I mean the pervasive and powerful values and beliefs that orient and inform the people of society. In the United States that religion is achievement, and it operates deeply in the psyche of Americans. Working-class Americans are no exception.

The Religion of Winning

The religion of winning can be stated this way: there is great opportunity for mobility; anyone can succeed; and people can move from the bottom to the very top of the society.

My Uncle Paul was not my only advisor. I remember a teacher in a classroom who once said to a group of about thirty south Mississippi girls and boys, "There is a ladder standing beside each desk in this room. If you want badly enough and if you will try hard enough, you can climb that ladder to the stars."

Sitting next to me in that room was a boy named Phillip whom I had known from the first grade. I knew he was smart. He always won when we played cowboys and Indians—even when he played an Indian. On the playground he won, but in class he lost. I think he lost in class because he did not have a bathtub in his house and he smelled. When he did bathe in a tub, he smelled like naphtha soap. By the time he was in the third grade, he believed he was dumb because he had been carefully taught to think so. The difference between Phillip and me was that he had physical talent and social limitations whereas I had social opportunity and physical limitations. It made no difference. We were both failures.

Phillip was the victim of a culture that prizes winning, that prizes being Number One. If there is a dominant value orientation of the United States people, if there is a civil religion, it is achievement. Winning is god, and adherents of the religion worship at a pyramidal altar where striving is endless because every success becomes a failure for not having done better. In the United States the true temple is the stadium, and people gather there by the thousands to watch in rapt and roaring tribute to the winner. Vince Lombardi was a prophet of the religion and captured its essence with the line, "Winning isn't everything, it's the only thing."

At the guts of this religion is the interplay of two beliefs. The first is individual freedom, and the second is equality of opportunity. The belief of individual freedom is more than a claim about personal liberty; it is a way of understanding and interpreting social life. Social issues and questions are seen in individual terms. Social problems are understood as the sum of individual actions or lack thereof. One is free to do and be as one wills.

The second belief, equality of opportunity, does not mean equal opportunity. It does not mean that all compete wth equal resources or on equal terms. It merely means that everyone has a right to compete, to struggle against others for advantaged positions.

My team used to play baseball against a team down in Bogue Chitto, Mississippi. Center field and right field were wide open. But in left field about 270 feet away from home plate in fair territory was a stand of pine trees. Those boys had more right-handed hitters than you could shake a stick at. It was strange, though. When one of them hit a ball into those pine trees, we hardly ever could find it in time to stop him from circling the bases. Yet when *we* hit one in there, they seemed to run in and come out throwing. What were home runs for them were only long singles for us. They had a magnetic capacity to find the baseball, or so it seemed.

The two teams had the equal right to compete. What we discovered, however, was that the other team had a sack of balls stashed out in the trees.

Individual freedom and equality of opportunity become destructive when they interact to become competitive individualism. People become lonely individuals by virtue of the fact that, at some level, everyone else is a rival. People become atomized as adversaries in virtually every dimension of life from the work place to the school, to the neighborhood, to the church—even in marriage.

More than that, the success or failure of a person is believed to be up to the individual. Implicitly this means that one is responsible for the degree of success or failure in one's own life and that people can be labeled winners and losers. There is hardly anything worse to call an American than "loser." Far worse than "sinner," "bigot," "crook," "thief," or "coward," a "loser" has committed the unforgivable sin. By the same token, there is no better name than "winner." Appropriate expressions of devotion are made to various religious and humanitarian virtues in the United States, but the most powerful inclusion/ exclusion principle (dividing the world into "them and us") across society is that of winners and losers.

One may question whether there has been a softening of winner religion in recent years. Daniel Yankelovich just completed a study of "the webs of significance Americans have spun around the shared meanings of self-fulfillment."[1] He found that the affluence of the twenty-five years following World War II led to major shifts in American culture. One of these is a change in what he calls the "giving/getting compact," that is, "the unwritten rules governing what we give in marriage, work, community and sacrifice for others, and what we expect in return."[2] Yankelovich found that many Americans, wearying of the rat race, are not so willing to *give* themselves to it in order to *get* traditional goals. Many are no longer willing to follow an ethic of self-denial. This shift has contributed to a powerful search for self-fulfillment among the American people, especially college-educated individuals under forty.

Yet while this search for self-fulfillment has affected most Americans, the power of winner religion is demonstrated in the persistent strength of what Yankelovich calls "social mobility" and the "competitive drive to success." Even in a time when the giant "geologic" plates of culture are moving, Yankelovich reports that competitiveness is "alive and well." He observes that

> People's image of the social hierarchy is not that of a ladder—what Disraeli called the "greasy pole." The dominant image is that of a giant arena in which Americans compete for an amazing variety of rewards, small and large, and where the rules for winning are clear and the contest is open.[3]

Thus, even in a time of significant change, Americans still believe in the reality of winner religion, confident that opportunities for "bettering oneself" exist in abundance.

What has changed is that Americans have turned from an ethic of self-denial to one of self-fulfillment. Their quest is for an intrinsically valuable and more deeply expressive life. Whether this shift will eventually have a significant impact on winner religion remains to be seen.

That Americans believe in winner religion is clear. It is a persistent faith. I believe that it is also an idolatrous one. Its god is destructive, especially for blue-collar people. There are at least four fundamental reasons why this is so.

The Contest for Dignity

One of the most destructive aspects of winner religion is that it places people in "a terrible contest for dignity, where we establish our own worth only by outpointing others in the crowded marketplace of respect."[4] People are in the spot of having to prove their worth, something that Christian thinkers—at least since Paul—claim cannot be done. And because this assumption pervades our culture, it supports the most thoroughgoing works of righteousness. Not only does it intensify whatever existential proclivities we humans have in such a direction, it also pervades our learned orientations and the ways we think, feel, and evaluate life.

In a small town where I once lived was a fellow whose name was Bernie. From the time he was seven or eight years old, he went up and down the streets of the town selling peanuts and popcorn and razor blades, and he yelled out, "Get your peanuts, popcorn, and razor blades!" He began to work when he was so small that he could walk under the swinging doors of the pool halls without scraping his back. He was a poor boy and worked at this job year after year. Soon he received the nickname of "Popcorn" or "Pops" for short.

When Bernie got to the eighth grade, he fell in love with a blond-haired, blue-eyed, "purdy"—not pretty, purdy—girl, as purdy as anybody he had ever seen. One day he asked her to go to the show (the movies).

"Well, Pops, I'd like to go. Let me ask my momma, and I'll let you know tomorrow because Momma has to approve all my dates."

The next day Pops could not find the girl. In fact, he did not see her until two days later. She had been dodging him.

"Well, what time am I picking you up?" Bernie asked.

"Pops, I'm not going."

"What do you mean you're not going?"

"I . . . just can't go."

"Why?"

"My momma won't let me."

"Why?"

"Well, I'd rather not say."

"Yeah, but I want to know why."

"Well, Pops, my momma thinks that you're not good enough for me."

It scorched him to the core, and he never forgot it.

The temptation is to be hard on the mother, but the mother had known what it was to struggle financially her whole life. Having a beautiful daughter in a majorette culture meant that her daughter had a chance to better herself. The mother's strategy worked. Beautiful and a nice person, the girl later married a decent fellow who happened to be the son of the man who owned one of the banks in town.

Meanwhile when Bernie turned fifteen, he bought a raggedy, old truck with the money he had saved and began hauling gladioli to New Orleans. Soon the old truck became a new truck, and the new truck became two trucks and then a rapidly expanding business. By the time Bernie was thirty, he was a millionaire, soon to become a multi-millionaire.

About twenty years after we had finished high school, I saw Bernie on the street one day. "Bernie, I sure am proud of you," I said after we had exchanged pleasantries.

"What about?"

"Well, I just hear you've done well, and I know how hard you've always worked."

"Aw, ain't done nothin'."

"Come on, now. Really, I hear you've done well."

"Aw, just strugglin' to make ends meet."

"Okay, have it your way. But, Bernie, I'll make you a bet," I said, knowing that he would wager which bird would fly off a telephone wire first.

"What?"

"I'll bet you don't put your money in Billy Wakely's bank."

"You'd lose that bet."

"What?"

"You'd lose the bet. I put every last nickel in that bank."

"Why would you do that?"

"Because I want that [bleep] countin' my money!"

There's something I like about that story. But there's also something haunting and crushing about it. Bernie had been slighted more than twenty-five years before, and the man was still trying to prove that he belonged in that town, that he was good enough to be there, and that he was somebody. While his success and wealth are very uncommon, his striving for dignity is pervasively American and human.

This contest for dignity takes a different direction for most women. They fit Jean Baker Miller's observation that women live out their lives by transfering their own hopes, needs, and goals onto others, chiefly their husbands and their children, if they have them.[5] This means that when men fail or do not realize their highest dreams—which is true often—then women blame themselves. It is a strange curse of sexism that keeps one gender of people distanced from full engagement with life and then generates self-blame for what happens there. That it is self-blame bears testimony to the power of the religion of winning.

Susan Ruach, a pastor in Indiana, points out an additional complexity for women in the religion of winning. The competition required in winner religion flies in the face of the role of women as nurturers. Thus a lot of women feel guilty about competing and so feel that they are not permitted to win. Many are socialized to believe that they cannot win. And living in a culture in which dignity is earned by winning—or so it is believed—and feeling that one's role is nurturance mean that one is defined out of the real action and that one's identity is a second-class identity. In this setting "second class" means "second gender."

Jean Lambert, a theologian at Saint Paul School of Theology, points out that women in an achievement culture wind up as losers in at least three ways. First, women are taught they *cannot* win and, hence, are devalued from the start. Second, their nurturance role implies that they *should not* win, and they are discounted again. Finally, when women realize that they want to win when they should not, they *feel guilty* and wind up losers a third time. As a result, women are valued mainly as bystanders, which is just one more form of being placed on a pedestal.

Cutting the Nerve of Social Criticism

John C. Raines points out a second reason for the destructiveness of winner religion: it cuts the nerve of social change by transforming social criticism into self-criticism, turning "the drive for social change into a passion for self-improvement."[6] On the one hand, as Raines points out, this accounts for the massive personal improvement industry, an avalanche of books, pamphlets, articles, and growth groups. On the other hand, it leads people to find the shape of their destiny not in social and historical forces but in themselves. This means that no matter what the obstacles, it is not society or historical circumstance that has determined people's fate, but people themselves, and they, therefore, are to blame. Hence there is no need to change society; the fault is in each person.

Each January a continuing education program at Saint Paul School of Theology is conducted for three weeks. The staff attempts to engage in theological reflection on a broad range of issues in the society and the church.

One day the staff and I spent a cloudy, dark afternoon talking with a woman who had spent most of her adult life working to stay off welfare, going back on it only when she was unable to do otherwise. We listened to her describe the tragedies that had befallen her son. He had a learning disability and a troubled history in school, plus peer pressures of their neighborhood, a constant fight with drug traffic, and a long history of involvement with the police. She told of the different jobs she had worked at, hoping to make a better life for him.

I have never heard a story more filled with objective social constraints on a family's life than the one she laid before us. Without special pleading, without once sounding a note of "poor me" she recounted one struggle after another. Finally, her son had gone to prison—where he was at that time.

Then, in the last minute she said it. She came to the conclusion no one expected, and yet we should have. "I know who's responsible. I ruined my son's life. When he was sixteen, I'm the one who bought him a leather jacket. When he was eighteen, I helped him buy a car for $200. I spoiled my son. I was not a good mother."

I have never seen a roomful of clergy so bereft of language. Her conclusion was intolerably oppressive because she had drawn the wrong one, and yet no one in the room felt adequate to counter it in a moment of such poignant, even though misplaced, self-blame. The moment had such weight of despair that no statement could lift it. The tragedy was too complete. Her experience was too permeated with failure, too locked up in a world without access. Mere talk could not speak to her condition.

Social change does not grow from self-blame and guilt, and self-improvement will never address the pattern of her life or her son's.

The Justification of Inequality

The religion of winning is destructive for a third reason: it justifies the structured inequality of the society. If one believes that motivation and effort lead to success, then, obviously, if one is successful, one deserves it. If one is not successful, one deserves that, too. Success is, therefore, the result of character, and failure derives from some personal inadequacy so that one is where one deserves to be. It is ironic that an ideology that grows from notions of freedom and equality winds up supporting the patterns of inequality that exist and taking away from people the legitimation to use their freedom and to change the social and political circumstances that constrain them.

The religion of winning supports structured inequality in one of the most powerful ways possible: it convinces people inwardly. To be sure, many people can name reasons for their fate, even empirically supported, objective reasons. But deep in their souls most Americans believe that losing is *their* fault and that they have received their just deserts. Scratch most Americans and beneath the skin you will find personal blame. This, then, preserves the status quo.

As a result people's rage at losing does not direct itself out-wardly—at the sources of inequality—but inwardly or at people nearest at hand. Sometimes they are spouses or children or minority groups or members of their own class. In the case of the last two, people do not identify with those beneath them in class and power hierarchies but rather compete against them, claiming that at least they are better than the "niggers" or the Indians or the "white trash."

Winner Religion and Reality

Finally, winner religion is destructive because it is not true. The factual claims made by the ideology fly in the face of social reality. Beth Vanfossen captures the essence of the situation:

> Like all ideologies, the dominant American ideology contains both value preachments and factual assertions. It preaches that individuals *should* work hard and strive to succeed in competition with others and asserts that, when they do, they *will* in fact be rewarded with success. The astounding feature of these beliefs is that most of them are contrary to the facts of social life. Oppor-tunity is not equal. It is restricted by racial, religious, ethnic, and sexual barriers, as well as by class differentials. Rags to riches is rare, and most mobility is minor. Intelligence is not related to income, nor is industriousness. Many jobs, particularly in the working class are dead-end; there are no avenues for ad-vancement. . . . Yet, the ideology defines success as a result of character and failure as a result of personal inadequacy.[7]

The result of this ideology, especially in terms of social strat-ification, is that it "encourages people to change their own particular position in the hierarchy."[8] One man said once to me, "I don't want to change it, I want to take advantage of it. Someday, I want to be at the top." He recently retired from the oil field, finishing his years of work as the foreman of a roust-about gang. To be sure, he lived better than most working-class people, but he never made it, even in his own terms.

The fact that the assumptions of winner religion are not valid is basic to understanding the life-style of blue-collar peo-ple because they are caught in the crunch of a culture with high expectations of success but they have sharply limited opportunities for achievement. Before turning to the life-styles of working-class people, I will look at sources of their social constraints. Basic to the social constraints is power. And for this reason the religion of winning is faulted by the reality of losing.

2

The Reality of Losing

I graduated from high school in 1953 and spent the summer working on a construction job at seventy-five cents an hour. By living at home and freeloading on my parents, I saved $300. This paid my tuition at L.S.U. the first semester, bought my books, and provided meals for the first month. At that point I was broke. The folks then "hocked" the house—an F.H.A.-financed one, purchased in 1939—to send me to school the rest of the year. I took a part-time job, but basically they supported me.

The next summer my buddy, Bobby Gaskill, and I got ready to go to the Kansas wheat fields to try to make more money. The day before we were to leave, my Dad told me, "I got you a job in the oil field making $2.25 an hour." That was all the money in the world at the time. With that pay I could work three months in the oil field and go to school on that money all the next year.

How did I get that job? When I was born, in the middle of the Depression, my dad was one of the fortunate people. He had three jobs: he delivered ice in the early morning, drove a school bus, and the rest of the day was a cobbler at Mr. Langford's Shoe Shop. When World War II broke out, he went to work in the shipyards in New Orleans. There he and my uncle J. L. made enough money to buy the McComb Eat Shop. For almost a year Dad made more money than he ever had, or ever would, by selling hamburgers and beer to young soldiers from Camp Shelby near Hattiesburg.

He had been a Mason and, with his newfound affluence became a Shriner. (I once asked him what a Shriner was; he replied, "He's just a drunk Mason, Son.") With that same affluence we soon left McComb and went back to Brookhaven where Dad bought the "13 Taxi Company," later to become the Yellow Cab Company with the only two-way radios in town. The cab business was never as lucrative as the eat shop, but Dad *was* a Shriner.

The way that I got the job was this. Dad ran into Doc Robbins, a physician and a Shriner, and told him I was going to Kansas the next day. "What on earth for?" Doc Robbins asked. When Dad told him, Doc suggested that I get a job with Bennie London at the California Company in the oil field west of town. When Dad said that he did not feel that he could ask London, Doc Robbins offered to do it, and I got the job.

The event was made possible by my father's membership in an influential group with plenty of contacts and resources. I discovered then that the rights and privileges one enjoys depend upon the power that the group or groups one belongs to can control and use.

I kept that job for the next four summers. The money I earned put me through college and my first year of graduate school and, I believe, changed the entire shape of my future. The "connections" that provided that job demonstrate the way power operates to benefit those in influential groups. Had my Dad not been a Shriner, that job would not have been available. Most other young white men would not have gotten the job without a connection. Had I been black or a woman no such opportunity would have existed.

We Americans have trouble with power. We do not like to talk about it. We take Lord Acton's aphorism with great seriousness: "Power tends to corrupt, and absolute power corrupts absolutely." In tension with this idea I have appreciated what a black activist said in Detroit in the midsixties: "Impotence corrupts, and absolute impotence corrupts absolutely."

In sociological literature one hears a good deal about "life chances" or "opportunity structures": the patterns of opportunities that people have in their lifetimes. The opportunity patterns are unequally distributed in the general population. Opportunity and power are closely linked. As we shall see, the groups to which one belongs, the part of the economy in which one works, and one's race and gender deeply affect one's chances and one's future.

The sketch that follows will illustrate some of the most determinative factors in a person's life. These factors constitute the objective context of the reality of losing.

Willie Mae Jackson

Willie Mae Jackson worked as a semi-skilled laborer in a small, family-owned factory in north Mississippi. The plant had moved south from Chicago to take advantage of the right-to-work laws of Mississippi. As a result of civil rights activity in the late fifties, the company attempted to avoid "any trouble" and simply hired three blacks. Mrs. Jackson was one of the three.

She worked for the company for twenty years and never received more than the minimum wage. Her pay increases occurred when the minimum wage increased. She was the breadwinner for her family through most of her adult life. Since the company had no pension program, she, retired, now lives on a social security check. This is modest because of her low wages in the factory and because she worked as a domestic, before the factory job, and did not pay into the social security program.

She had been a disciplined employee: punctual, loyal, and hardworking. Possessing a good sense of humor, she got along well with others in the plant. The white people said she was "a good one." "If all the colored people were like Willie Mae, things would be fine."

Mrs. Jackson will continue to be poor, as she has been

throughout the last sixty-five years. Her children help her, but their own circumstances will not permit them to do much. She lives on East Chicasaw Street in an old house she still rents "from Mister Robert Harrison." She will stay there as long as she can. "When I have to, I will go and live with my children in Houston."

Power and the Dual Economy

In order to understand the structural realities that have determined the fate of Willie Mae Jackson, we have to look at the emergence of the multinational corporation (MNC) and with it the coming of a dual economy. The MNC is a major, operative factor in a thoroughgoing transformation of the global economy and has a pervasive impact on the working-class people of the entire world.

What began as an attempt by corporations to develop and control supplies of raw materials has become in fact a massive growth in production on an international scale.[1] The MNC transcends the nation state. The MNC, by its global reach into rich and poor countries, orchestrates its advantage by exploiting raw materials in one country, cheap labor in another, high market demand in a third, and beneficent tax climates in yet another. Thus, the MNC is able to take advantage of the buyers' markets and the sellers' markets of the world.

One structural result of the MNC is the development of primary and secondary sectors in the economy and, with those, the development of primary and secondary labor markets.[2] People who work for MNCs are in the primary labor market. They represent a small fraction of the labor force of the world and, by and large, benefit from the present economic change. Typically, people enter the primary job market at an early age and have some opportunity for career development. They work for large public or private corporations or for industries in which good job conditions are bargained for by powerful unions. The jobs require high skills and pay well.

The core [primary sector] economy includes those industries that comprise the muscle of American economic and political power. . . . Entrenched in durable manufacturing, the construction industries, the firms in the core economy are noted for high productivity, high profits, intensive utilization of capital, high incidence of monopoly elements, and a high degree of unionization. What follows normally from such high characteristics are high wages. The automobile, steel, rubber, aluminum, aerospace and petroleum industries are ranking members of this part of the economy. Workers who are able to secure employment in these industries are, in most cases, assured of relatively high wages and better than average working conditions and fringe benefits. . . .[3]

In the private or secondary sector, supply and demand set the wages of workers. Jobs are less secure. There is more turnover and less chance for career development. These workers are far more marginal and expendable. These are the people most hard hit by unemployment.

Beyond the fringes of the core economy lies a set of industries that lack almost all of the advantages normally found in center firms. Concentrated in agriculture, nondurable manufacturing, retail trade, and subprofessional services, the peripheral industries are noted for their small firm size, labor intensity, low profits, low productivity, intensive product market competition, lack of unionization, and low wages. Unlike core sector industries, the periphery lacks the assets, size, and political power to take advantage of economics of scale or to spend large sums on research and development.[4]

Obviously a major imbalance of power exists beteen the primary and secondary sectors of the economy. Research indicates that these sectoral differences are fateful for the opportunities and experiences of blue collarites. People who work in the secondary sector earn on an average over $3,000 *less* per year than people in the primary sector.[5] About one third of this difference is due to the characteristics of the workers; *for example* workers in the secondary sector are often less skilled or less educated than those in the primary sector. Yet "there are persistent sectoral differences in economic outcomes which cannot be explained by the racial, sexual, human capital, or occupational characteristics of their respective labor forces."[6]

Interestingly enough, Beck found that white males in the secondary sector had an earnings disadvantage of over $5,000, which means that "the economic impact of the sectoral distinction is *more* pronounced among white males than among workers in general." About $1,000 of this difference is due to the characteristics of the workers. The remaining $4,000 difference is a sectoral one.[7]

A final note. One important factor in the dual economy is whether one lives in a rural, small town, or metropolitan area. Since core sector industries are usually located in metropolitan centers, people who want the power and the pay need to live there and be employed there. Thus, first of all, Willie Mae Jackson's fate was determined by the facts that she spent her entire life working in the secondary sector in a nonmetropolitan area.

Power and Organization

When there is high demand for scarce skills and services and the possessors and providers of these skills and services are organized cohesively, the skilled workers will wield considerable power and be able to demand high pay. This is true of unions and various professional organizations, among others.

About one third of the nonagricultural work force in the United States is unionized. Mining, construction, manufacturing, and transportation industries are usually highly unionized while agriculture, the distributive trades, and government work have been less so. Even though the power of unions is checked by employers, unions make a difference in the wages that workers receive. Studies show that average union wages are approximately 10 to 15 percent higher than nonunion wages.[8]

The power of professional associations is also a part of this picture. Friedman and Kuznets found that medical associations have been able to raise the pay for physicians' services by restricting the number of M.D.'s coming out of medical schools. H. G. Lewis estimated that airline pilots' associations have increased their members' pay by some 20 to 34 percent.[9]

The fact that Willie Mae Jackson spent her life working first as a domestic and then in a nonunion shop meant that she never was a member of a strong organization that represented her interests and bargain , for higher pay. Her wages never exceeded the hourly minimum and, while she was a domestic, never reached that minimum.

Power and Job Markets

Many people do not realize that there are a number of different job markets within the United States economy. These job markets radically affect a person's income, mobility, prestige, and opportunity. Hence the imbalances of power among these job markets is a third fateful reality for working-class people.

One blue-collar man said to me, "I've got to get out of these poverty jobs and get into something that pays well." His comment reflects the findings of Miller and Form who have classified job markets into five types and contend that "these markets are social as well as economic phenomena and tend to parallel economic classes."[10] While these markets are not mutually exclusive, nevertheless distinctions among them can be made on the basis of a number of characteristics: occupational makeup, power to determine income, amount of income, "degree of particularism in setting income," fringe benefits and nonmoney income, and resources for changing income levels.[11]

The five job markets are as follows:

1. *The self-controlled market* is made up of the owners and managers of large corporations who make decisions about incomes not only for others but for themselves as well. If a corporation has moderate prosperity, the owners and managers have considerable leeway in setting their own salaries. They tend to assign themselves the highest incomes they can while still being consistent with company policy and the fiscal policy which they themselves set for the company. Here they are governed by the enterprise's economic well-being and their own self-restraint. They also receive the highest noncash payments available and experience no unemployment.[12]

2. *Traditional markets* are composed of doctors, lawyers, plumbers, and carpenters, that is "the old-line independent professionals, independent artisans, and service workers . . . [those] in occupations which have traditions and institutions to maintain them." They "have skill monopolies and an ethic

dealing with their relations." Incomes in this job market vary considerably but tend to be moderate to high. The incomes are derived from fees and, to some degree, take into account the client's ability to pay (or the coverage given by the client's insurance). Control of entry into the occupation and professional associations constitutes a basic source of power.[13]

3. *The administered market* is made up of the big governmental and business bureaucracies. While containing the full sweep of occupations, they are composed primarily of white-collar workers. Salaries are carefully graduated and tend to avoid the high and low incomes of the "free market." Sometimes higher salaries are exchanged by employees for greater job security and nonsalary benefits. Organizing and bargaining activity are often restricted, and political participation is often limited in such bureaucracies.[14]

4. *The contested market* is one in which labor unions "bargain with management to fix wage rates for classes of employees. The power to set wages is circumscribed by the strength of the parties, the general economic situation, and some traditional forces." Contested market incomes tend to run from moderate to low. Because of the economic insecurity of most workers, unions attempt to offset the negative effects of market forces.[15]

5. *The free or marginal market* exists "where individuals and economic units are not organized, so that the free play of economic forces is permitted." Typically this job market is made up of jobs in small retail stores, farms, and small businesses. It includes farm laborers, domestics, and casual workers whose skills and wages are low, whose wages reflect supply and demand. Union organization is virtually nonexistent. "Typically, the economic units are small and the employees tend to be marginal. The ideal type here might be the small retailer or manufacturer who is on the edge of economic survival, hiring workers who do not find a place in other more secure markets."[16]

Blue-collar workers are found primarily in the traditional, the contested, and the free job markets. "Blue-collar aristocrats," as they are sometimes called, are more likely to be found in the traditional and contested markets because in these one finds the largest portions of well-paid workers. Most unionized workers are, of course, in the contested market. It is important to remember here, however, that only about a third of blue-collar workers are organized and that a significant number of them are not in strong unions. The majority of working-class people hold jobs in the free market. Some here receive moderate pay, but this is mainly the job market of the marginal worker, of the poor, and of the dispossessed. It is also the job market most closely associated with the secondary sector of the economy and, hence, subject to the powerlessness of it. Willie Mae Jackson spent her life in the free job market.

Power, Race, and Gender

Two more groupings that are enormously fateful for working-class people are those of race and gender. The median family income of blacks is about 60 percent of the family incomes of whites. Blacks earn less money in every category of employment because they hold the lowest-paying jobs in each category.[17] O. D. Duncan concluded that at least a third

> of the difference in average income between blacks and whites arises because Negro and white men in the same line of work, with the same amount of formal schooling, with equal ability, from families of the same size and the same socioeconomic level, simply do not draw the same wages and salaries.[18]

Fully employed women earn about 60 percent of what fully employed men do. Beth Vanfossen observes that this "does not represent much of an improvement over biblical times, at least according to Leviticus 27, wherein it is indicated that adult females were worth thirty shekels and adult males fifty shekels."[19]

Women are usually employed in lower-paying jobs than men. Women work in an "internal labor market" as Louise Kapp Howe has described it. This is the job structure within a company "which is typically as segregated by sex as is the labor market as a whole."[20] This leads economist Marina Whitman to call it the "'employment ghetto' of women's work."[21] Women are waitresses, seamstresses, secretaries, bookkeepers, nurses, and teachers.

> Although they are represented in highly paid occupations, over 73 percent of women workers are employed as salespersons, clerks, semiskilled factory workers, or service workers (compared to 36 percent of the men). . . . These differences exist in spite of the fact that women in America receive about the same amount of education as do men.[22]

Here, again, Willie Mae Jackson was the wrong race and the wrong gender. It meant that she spent her working life in an internal job market—an employment ghetto—reserved for women and for blacks.

Power and Fate

I have tried to suggest that a person's rights and privileges depend upon the power of the groups to which that person belongs. More specifically, I have tried to suggest that fateful realities of power are determined by a person's sector of the economy, labor and professional organizations, job markets, and racial and gender characteristics.

One might still argue, I suppose, that these structures simply filter out the best people and that racial and sexual character- istics are mainly a matter of cultural lag that will soon be overcome. However, Beth Vanfossen, in summarizing research on the importance of structural variables versus those of human capital (characteristics of individuals), concludes:

> . . . structural variables are far more important in determining blue-collar income than are the personal characteristics of edu- cation, vocational training, experience, and employment history. Fifty percent of the variation in incomes is related to structural variables, while only 18 percent is related to human capital var- iables. . . . In concrete terms, the analysis showed on the basis of 1972 income data that to be male increased one's income by about $4,000; to be employed in the primary sector, by almost $2,000; to be located in a major metropolitan area, by about $1,200; and to belong to a union, by $1,100.[23]

Moreover, a study by Wachtel and Betsey has similar results. Including race as a variable, they discovered that race was an even more important indicator of income than gender.[24]

These then are the major structural factors that set the destiny of Willie Mae Jackson. Her race, her gender, and her work in the free market of the secondary sector in the economy are the structural reasons she never made more than the minimum wage. These realities transcended the qualities she had as a hard-working, cooperative, and efficient employee.

The economy does not work the way Adam Smith said it would. It is not simply the workings of competing individuals pursuing their self-interest amidst the vicissitudes of supply and demand. The *homo economicus* of Adam Smith is reductionistic. Humans seek not only economic self-interests but power as well. Because of this will to power, human groups, not just individuals, organize and form concentrations of power and use them to resist market forces. The truth of the matter is that no group willingly becomes subject to the forces of supply and demand. Rather, each group tries to make its competitor subject to them. Charles Dickens captured the true essence of free enterprise: "'God for us all and every man for himself!' said the elephant as he danced among the chickens."

One sociologist has said that Adam Smith's economic vision of the market system is the perfect model, a vision without weakness or flaw, *until one puts it in a human society*.[25] There is found, not some beneficent invisible hand, but the struggle for power, and concentrations of power, as I have shown, determine the fates of individuals and their families and construct the palaces of privilege and hovels of deprivation.

Americans have a way of thinking about everything in terms of their own inner subjectivity. They believe they can dispose of problems by changing their attitudes, by thinking positively, or by coming at things with an open mind. Unfortunately there are shoals of *objective* inequality that shipwreck the most positive people in the world if they get caught in the wrong channel.

Recent Trends

The structural factors that so radically affected Mrs. Jackson's life have a more intense impact because of recent trends in the American economy. In the winter of 1983 the United States was in a deep recession. Reaching well over 10 percent, the unemployment rate was the highest since the Great Depression, and this figure did not include "discouraged workers." People lined up by the tens of thousands to apply for two hundred jobs at a plant in Milwaukee. Soup kitchens began again in communities where they had not existed for fifty years. Human services were cut back to increase military spending. The people hit hardest by these events were the poor and working-class people of the country.

Perhaps these trends are cyclical. Some economists believe that the country is now turning a corner. Inflation has slowed; interest rates are down, construction has started again, and auto sales are up; inchoate signs of a rise in productivity are appearing. These positive notes are counterpointed by the projection of immense, unprecedented national budget deficits. Still, some say that in a year or two or three the economy will be back on its feet—scant comfort to a working-class person who has been unemployed for six months already.

Yet, even if the economy begins to improve, certain trends spell out an ominous future for blue-collar Americans. Richard W. Gillett has outlined four such trends. The first is the "deindustrialization of the American economy," defined by Barry Bluestone and Bennett Harrison as "a widespread, systematic disinvestment in the nation's productive capacity." The basic ingredient in this deindustrialization is the diversion of financial resources, plants, and equipment "from productive investment in our basic national industries into unproductive speculation, mergers, acquisitions, and foreign investment. Left behind are shuttered factories, displaced workers, and a newly emerging group of ghost towns." Bluestone and Harrison estimate that 30 to 50 million jobs have been lost in the country as a direct consequence of private disinvestment by United States businesses.[26]

As heavy industry declines, the service sector is expanding rapidly. About three-fourths of the workers losing their jobs in heavy industry are finding new ones in the service sector, typically for considerably less pay. The other fourth of the workers remain unemployed because service sector jobs are not numerous enough to replace those lost in heavy industry.

The second trend is the transportation and communications revolution of the past ten to fifteen years that has led to the development of a global economy in which multinational corporations manage and produce on a worldwide scale.

> Huge cargo aircraft can now fly virtually an entire factory halfway across the globe, while decisions as to how fast that new factory assembly line must operate, what its workers should be paid and what profit is to be made are based on data from the corporation's global computers back in Connecticut or New York.[27]

As a result many multinationals move plants overseas or to the dominantly nonunion United States South where labor costs are much cheaper and profitability greater. It should be understood that most of these closed plants were not unprofitable; they simply did not meet the profit expectations of the corporations.

The third major trend is the acceleration of automation in plants and offices. This trend will spell further job losses for many workers.

> ... General Motors has calculated that in a decade 90 percent of its machine tools will be computerized. ... Another company has estimated that robots can economically replace two-thirds of all production painters and one-half of all production welders—resulting in about 1 million jobs lost.[28]

Finally, work is becoming increasingly de-skilled. The range of work that people do becomes narrower so that skills are diminished and the work itself becomes increasingly meaningless, alienating, and dehumanizing.[29] Concommitant with such de-skilling is a loss of power by workers because they become as interchangeable as the parts workers handle on assembly lines. When skill is diminished, so is one's capacity to bargain and operate from a position of strength.

These four trends cause personal devastation to working-class people and their communities. And labor unions seem to

be losing their position and strength in the society as a coun-
tervailing power to business and industry.

It is quite evident that these trends represent a growing
inequality in the United States with the result that the reality
of losing deepens. These objective factors have a subjective
impact. I turn now to that, to find out what the experience of
losing is like.

3

The Experience of Losing

It is not enough to talk about the objective factors in the reality of losing, those that condition and shape life for people. It is also important to look at the reality of losing in terms of what it feels like, how it is experienced.

One way to look at social class and, therefore, at working-class people is to see how power affects the relationships among them. Randall Collins has defined power as "the experience of giving orders and receiving ritual deference."[1] We will look at giving orders and ritual deference as the first step in understanding the experience of class and the encounters of blue-collar people in their everyday existence.

Giving and Taking Orders

Collins contends that the giving and taking of orders is one way to measure class. The people who basically *give* orders and take very few are upper class. Those who both give *and* take orders are middle class. And those who give few orders and mostly *take* them are lower class. Collins observes that "power relations, situations of giving and taking orders, seem to be the most important behavior-shaping experiences in the world of work."[2]

For three summers I played softball with a group of auto-workers in Kansas City. On the team was a guy named Dick. We made him the manager of the team because we did not want him to play. However, we usually had only nine men, and he was often "pressed into service." He was the worst ball player I ever saw who played regularly. Of the first eleven chances he had one year, he missed ten of them. He knew that he couldn't play ball, but he wanted to so badly.

One night our team was at bat, and I was sitting on the bench with Scoots, an over-forty player like me but an exceptionally fine shortstop and hitter. Dick was across the field, coaching at third base. After one batter flied out, Dick suddenly realized that it was his turn to bat. All the way across the diamond Dick started yelling at us, "Hey, one of you guys, get over here! It's my turn to hit!"

Scoots muttered angrily to me, "Hell! He doesn't mean hit, he means swing. Listen to him! He talks like he's the boss. He ain't nothin'. *He works on the line just like I do.* You'd think he was the damned boss!"

What came through so clearly was not that Scoots resented Dick's inability to play ball but that Scoots resented Dick's giving orders like a boss. Scoots was mature as a person and never got on Dick about his errors, a virtue not practiced by others. When Dick blew a play, Scoots would smile and shout encouragement to him. What apparently was not forgivable was for Dick to make demands, especially on a ball field, the place where a man's ability was self-evident and where one man did not give orders to another.

The work of Kohn and Schooler fits here and extends Collins's views about giving and taking orders. The focus of their study is on occupational conditions, "particularly those that are conducive to, or restrictive of, the exercise of self-direction in work."[3] They found that middle-class men (it *was* a study of men) were more likely to be in jobs that provide opportunity for self-direction; that is, jobs in which they can use initiative, thought, and independent judgment. Whereas blue-collar men were in work roles that require conformity to external authority.

Self-direction was discovered to be important and desirable not only with respect to work but also in other realms of life. In the case of fathers, the higher their class position, the more they valued self-direction for their children and the less they valued characteristics of conformity to external authority. Kohn and Schooler found also that the higher the men's class position, the more they valued self-direction for themselves both in thought and in action.

Moreover, self-direction on the job affected attitudes toward work. Men of higher social class valued intrinsically satisfying work, and blue-collar men attached more importance to extrinsic factors, such as "pay, fringe benefits, the supervisor, co-workers, the hours of work, how tiring the work is, job security, and not being under too much pressure."[4]

Among other findings they discovered that the lower the social-class positions of the men, "the more likely they are to feel that morality is synonymous with obeying the letter of the law; the less trustful of their fellow [humans] they are; and the more resistant they are to innovation and change." Moreover, they found "the strongest correlation, by a wide margin," of social class is with authoritarian conservatism; that is, the lower their social class, the more rigidly conservative the men were about human beings and institutions and the less they tolerated nonconformity.[5]

How the men saw themselves is of interest. Kohn and Schooler found that the relationship of class to self-conception was not as strong as the relationship of class to social orientation (how people view the external world). The findings were still consistent in that the

> higher the men's social class position, the more self-confidence and the less self-deprecation they express; the greater their sense of being in control of the forces that affect their lives; the less beset by anxiety they are; and the more independent they consider their ideas to be.[6]

Among the conditions of work that contribute to or diminish self-direction, three are critical according to Kohn and Schooler: a) the degree of supervision; b) the substance of the work, whether it requires initiative, thought, and independent judgment; and c) whether the work has sufficient complexity to allow for a variety of approaches. While each of these conditions is determinative of self-direction in work, the substance of the work is the far more important condition.

> Work with "data" or with "people" is more likely to require initiative, thought and judgment than is work with "things". . . . Thus, occupational self-direction is most probable when men spend some substantial amount of their working time doing complex work with data or with people.[7]

The work of Kohn and Schooler demonstrates the pervasive influence of giving and taking orders in one's work encounters. As dehumanizing as it can be to take orders under close supervision, the evidence here suggests that routinized work, with its pattern of responsibilities imposed by the use of machinery, can be even more demanding. This qualifies somewhat Collins's understanding of encounters of giving and taking orders. People also have such encounters with "things"—with machines, assembly lines, procedures—and these, apparently, can be more imperative than people. However, workers with "things" are under the orders of people.

Blue-collar women are no exception when it comes to taking orders. Their situation is worse. "The working-class woman in particular remains in a network of subordination—in the home and in the workplace as a woman, socioeconomically and culturally as working-class."[8]

Louise Kapp Howe's conversation with a beautician captures this subordination at home.

> [Kapp:] "You and Avis and Marianne are the three in the shop who have children?"
>
> [Beautician:] "Yes, and for some of us it's difficult. Most of the girls they have cars, and they can go wherever they feel like. I can't. I have a daughter and she's at that age where she needs attention, and if I'm not there to give it to her she's not going to get it. My husband really doesn't care about kids. And my husband also takes the car, so I'm not able to work late like some of the other girls."

[Kapp:] "But he comes home early, around four o'clock you told me. He could pick you up?"

[Beautician:] "Yeah, he could but he doesn't like to be inconvenienced."[9]

Jackie, another beautician, captures the resentment of a subordinate position and taking orders:

"I was taught to do the competition hairdos, the fancy sets and good coloring jobs, and I used to love haircuts. Shampoos don't really bother me and I don't mind washing tint off or taking permanent wave rods out—it's just time consuming. But when I do those things some of the ladies are so rude I get so I have to walk away to cool down. I really thought I was a patient person before, but now if my attitude is gruff toward a lot of women, which I guess it is, it's because I really resent those other things I have to do. . . ."[10]

Perhaps the most telling illustration of the feeling that women have about taking orders can be found in Walshok's work on blue-collar women who are entering jobs previously held by men. These are jobs such as welding, carpentry, mechanics, plumbing, or electrical work. While some of this employment would not be attractive from a middle-class point of view and while it involves a great deal of order taking, the women in these jobs express high appreciation for their work. These "skilled blue-collar jobs represent a marvelous opportunity to do something more challenging, interesting, and autonomous than the limited occupations traditionally open to women." Walshok points out that one can understand the significance of such work "only by understanding its relationship to the previous paid and unpaid work experiences of women in American society."[11]

She goes on to say,

Our findings suggest that women in skilled blue-collar jobs are extremely, even surprisingly, satisfied. They judge their present opportunities different than do men or well-educated women. It is not only because of the better money that they are satisfied. It is also because of the challenging qualities the nontraditional work experience offers, in contrast to traditional women's work. Whether domestic or paid, traditional women's work has become increasingly diminished and trivialized in urban-industrial societies, and no longer offers these women what they want." [12]

Lillian Rubin writes,

> There is, perhaps, no greater testimony to the deadening and deadly quality of the tasks of the housewife than the fact that so many women find pleasure in working at jobs that by almost any definition would be called alienated labor—low-status, low-paying dead-end work made up of dull, routine tasks. . . . [13]

Deference and Demeanor

Ritual deference and demeanor are yet another dimension of the experience of class. Here, again, Randall Collins's view is instructive. For Collins, "rituals" are "normal encounters among people in everyday life in which they create, sustain, and change society." That is, in Collins's view, society is constructed—it is *actually built*—in the small, everyday encounters people have as persons. Even rituals of greeting—"Hi, how are you?" "Fine, yourself?" "Oh, just fine, thank you."—are occasions in which people fabricate society. Collins says about his point of view: "My approach . . . understands social structure as something enacted from moment to moment; reality is whatever people negotiate a belief in." [14]

Among the most fateful of these encounters are those between superiors and subordinates in which deference is given and received by means of demeanor. Deference is shown in the way people use talk, gestures, and postures to give or to elicit respect from others. "Demeanor" means "bearing, the way people comport themselves," that is, the manner in which people use gestures, body language, and talk. It refers to the attitudes of "looking up to" someone or "looking down on" them. Along with giving and taking orders deference is the stuff of which the experience of class is made.

Obviously, who is on top and who is on bottom in these rituals of deference and demeanor depend upon the distribution of factors, such as wealth, power, and the resources of personal and organizational contacts. I remember well a man I worked with in the oil field who was charismatic, articulate, bright, and a privilege to be around. His jokes and conversation kept our minds off the heavy labor we did. He was a Mississippi Zorba. *But* when the big boss came out on the job, he became quiet, unsure of himself, and assumed a posture in which he basically looked at his feet.

Such is the way that deference and demeanor work in the experience of class. Imagine, then, if you will, the myriad occasions in everyday life in which deference and demeanor are at work. It is in this ecology of interpersonal contacts that class is experienced.

Illustrations of this abound in the literature of social stratification. Elliot Liebow did a participant-observation study of black street-corner men in Washington, D.C. in the early sixties. In his book, *Tally's Corner*, he reports a conversation he had with Tally, a cement finisher. It was summer, the peak earning season for Tally. He was bringing home "a lot of bread." But he needed more than money.

[Tally:] "You know that boy came in last night? That Black Moozlem? That's what I ought to be doing. I ought to be in his place."

[Liebow:] "What do you mean?"

[Tally:] "Dressed nice, going to [night] school, got a good job."

[Liebow:] "He's not better off than you, Tally. You make more than he does."

[Tally:] "It's not the money. [Pause] It's position, I guess. He's got position. When he finish school he gonna be a supervisor. People respect him. . . . Thinking about people with position and education gives me a feeling right here [pressing his fingers into the pit of his stomach]."

[Liebow:] "You're educated, too. You have a skill, a trade. You're a cement finisher. You can make a building, pour a sidewalk."

[Tally:] "That's different. Look, can anybody do what you're doing? Can anybody just come up and do your job? Well, in one week I can teach you cement finishing. You won't be as good as me 'cause you won't have the experience but you'll be a cement finisher. That's what I mean. Anybody can do what I'm doing and that's what gives me this feeling. [Long pause] Suppose I like this girl. I go over to her house and I meet her father. He starts talking about what he done today. He talks about operating on somebody

and sewing them up and about surgery. I know he's a doctor
'cause of the way he talks. Then she starts talking about what
she did. Maybe she's a boss or a supervisor. Maybe she's a lawyer
and her father says to me, 'And what do you do, Mr. Jackson?'
[Pause] You remember at the courthouse, Lonny's trial? You and
the lawyer was talking in the hall? You remember? I just stood
there listening. I didn't say a word. You know why? 'Cause I didn't
even know what you was talking about. That's happened to me
a lot."

[Liebow:] "Hell, you're nothing special. That happens to every-
body. Nobody knows everything. One man is a doctor, so he talks
about surgery. Another man is a teacher, so he talks about books.
But doctors and teachers don't know anything about concrete.
You're a cement finisher and that's your specialty."

[Tally:] "Maybe so, but when was the last time you saw anybody
standing around talking about concrete?"[15]

The significance of deference and demeanor in interpersonal
contacts is manifested throughout Tally's conversation. As he
saw himself in comparison with the Black Muslim and at Lonny's trial, he experienced himself as subordinate and inferior.
Even in his imagination he saw himself in a subordinate relationship to a woman who was a lawyer or a supervisor and
whose father was a surgeon. Deference and demeanor are rituals people enact in interpersonal encounters and in intra-
psychic conversations.

Louise Kapp Howe captures the plight of "pink-collar" workers in their struggles with deference and demeanor. Howe
observes that working conditions and pay were the most press-
ing problems on the mind of the women she interviewed. Yet,

the general public's lack of respect for and recognition of their
work, both because of class and sexist prejudice, was a subject
that did come up spontaneously again and again. Particularly
among the young women.

Suzy at the beauty shop: *People won't tell you this, they think we
don't know what they're feeling, but a lot of them think we're cheap,
think we're lower class.*

Jeanne King, waitress: *Oh, yeah. Most people on the outside look
down on you. Middle class people I'm talking about. [This] is the
thing I object to about this job more than anything else.*

Jackie at the beauty shop: *They think their shit is cleaner than yours. Well, I could spit on them.*

Ingrid at Tony's restaurant: *Some people say that what we do is unskilled work. All I can say is that they should come work here at lunchtime during the middle of the week and see how well they do.*[16]

The Experience of Failure

A third aspect of the "feel" of class is the experience of failure. It is a persistent experience for people in the lower end of the class structure. When they look at TV shows with program sets of expensive homes and the good life, when they compare their expectations with their dreams, when they witness someone that is Number One, they taste the experience of failure.

Of course, all human beings fail. Failure is inevitable in human affairs, but it creates powerful devastation in a winner culture. In fact, it is a good question whether there are any real winners. Do we not all wind up "losers"? Every victory seems to fade into some new striving in which the hollowness of success generates the impulse to climb again with the hope that some new height will bring satisfaction.

For people in the lower end of the class structure the experience of failure is even more pervasive. There the comparison of self with others, especially with the "winners," can be drawn most sharply. It is difficult to estimate the enormity of the impact of failure on lower-class people.

For some time social scientists contended that working-class and poor people had their own distinct cultures, different than those of the mainstream or middle class. More recent research, however, suggests that another explanation is in order. In his study of black street-corner men, Elliot Liebow contends that they do "not constitute a distinctive cultural pattern 'with an integrity of its own.' It is rather the cultural model of the larger society as seen through the prism of repeated failure."[17]

One passage in Liebow is especially poignant. It describes the experience of failure for the black street-corner man in job, marriage, and family.

Although he wants to get married, he hedges on his commitment from the very beginning because he is afraid, not of marriage itself, but of his own ability to carry out his responsibilities as husband and father. His own father failed and had to "cut out," and the men he knows who have been or are married have also failed or are in the process of doing so. He has no evidence that he will fare better than they and much evidence that he will not. However far he has gone in school he is illiterate or almost so; however many jobs he has had or how hard he has worked, he is essentially unskilled. Armed with models who have failed, convinced of his own worthlessness, illiterate and unskilled, he enters marriage and the job market with the smell of failure all around him.[18]

The experience of failure is devastating for women as well. Later on I shall report more fully on Mary Walshok's research on blue-collar women in jobs traditionally held by men. Her findings underscore the key role that the experience with failure has on the capacity of women to stay in nontraditional blue-collar work roles. Women who had undergone devastating trauma and failure in their early lives were least likely to stay in nontraditional jobs, whereas women who had faced serious trouble while they were young, but with support, risk, and effort had made it, were most likely to hold onto their jobs.

The experience of failure, pervasive in an achievement-oriented culture and compounded for the poor and the near poor, stalks blue-collar working people. It looms in people's fears and contemplation of the future. To be defined as a loser and to accept that definition for oneself is as close to hell as anything that there is in a winner culture.

I know a man named Jim Case who had heard that a moving company was interested in training people to drive large vans. If one was eligible and satisfactorily completed the training program of a few weeks, the company would help the driver finance the purchase of a rig. The driver would then be part of the company's nationwide moving business. The work also paid well, which was what first attracted Jim.

He bought a few new clothes and drove a thousand miles to the company's training center. Somehow he had not taken note of the educational requirement. While he was and is an able and bright person with plenty of experience, Jim has only a fifth-grade education. When he filled out an information sheet upon his arrival, they told him that they were sorry and that there must have been some misunderstanding, but they simply could not take anyone into the program who had only a fifth-grade education. He got into his car and drove all the way back home.

A courageous man with a keen sense of humor, he told the story on himself to his friends and family. He laughed at himself for being so foolish. Yet even in his laughter, his pain was so intense that I remember the difficulty I had keeping my eyes on him as he told the story.

In sum, the experience of class for working-class people includes taking orders, giving respect, and experiencing failure. These come in countless encounters with other people, with machines, with memories, and even fantasies. In a winner culture, people who know the reality and the feel of losing still have to live. And they live under such conditions the way one might suspect: by struggling and adapting, by rationalization and compensative life-styles, and some by just plain giving up. We will now turn to the ways of living that working-class people adopt to survive in the crunch between the religion of winning and the reality of losing.

Part II

Blue-Collar Life-Styles

4

Blue-Collar Winners

"You can tell what people really believe by how they act and what they do."

The purpose of Part II is to demonstrate how *incorrect* the above statement is. The relationship between values and behavior is not direct for the simple reason that people always value and behave in a *context*. The degree to which they are able to live out what they truly believe depends, in great part, on the context in which they find themselves and the opportunities it offers.

This is certainly true for blue-collar people. We cannot understand their life-styles as manifestations of the religion of winning unless we see these beliefs in the context of the reality of losing. Such a context makes a difference between people's valued preferences and their realistic expectations.

Wan Sang Han maintains that one's expectations are strongly affected by how much opportunity one has. Thus, while people's *preferences* reflect the societal emphasis upon success and achievement, their *expectations* represent a far more realistic assessment of their class circumstances and a consequent adjustment of their hopes. Wan Sang Han hence distinguishes between a "circumstance-free wish" and a "circumstance-bound expectation."

Utilizing this distinction, Wan Sang Han interviewed 465 students from three high schools in metropolitan Atlanta. The students represented families of working-class people, lower white-collar people, managers, and professionals. Han found that all (or most) shared common *wishes* but that their expectations revealed a divergence from their wishes that increased as students of lower status expressed their awareness of restricted realities. It seemed to be quite clear in these students' minds that what they wished for and what they might realistically expect were two quite different things.[1]

Thus one must not confuse actual behavior, which is often adaptive to circumstances, with the cultural preferences of people. That is, while the United States culture is characterized by high valuations of success, people find it difficult to be successful in the face of sharply unequal life chances. This means that a good deal of behavior will quite likely be adaptive and compensative. Hence a deeper understanding of blue-collar life-styles requires an appreciation of the disjunction between cultural values and life chances.

What then is the outcome for people who live in the crunch between achievement myths and blue-collar realities? How does that conflict affect their life-styles? Obviously, blue-collar people live in several different contexts. Some have jobs with better pay and benefits than others who struggle to survive. Any attempt to characterize the achievement myths' responses of working-class people must reflect these differences. What follows is a simplification, but I hope to convey something of the complexity of blue-collar life-styles.

Basically, four general patterns are described. These four patterns come from a number of important studies. I use them here not so much to place working-class people in boxes as to illuminate patterns of behavior that do exist. Moreover, a blue-collar family may be characterized by one pattern at one time in its life, but through the force of circumstances, it may live out another life-style during another period. This is to say that people are not frozen into a life-style, although, of course, some people live out their lives exemplifying one life-style.

Blue-Collar Winner Men

The first group is blue-collar winner men. LeMasters calls them blue-collar aristocrats in his study of highly paid workers at a working-class tavern. He reports, "I never heard a single man say that he hated his work—or even disliked it."[2] The pay and the benefits were good. The work was not monotonous, and they had freedom to move around and to exercise judgment on the job. The men had the security of union membership and seniority. Working outdoors was important to them, and they took considerable pride in the buildings they helped to construct and other jobs they held.

LeMasters found that the major problem in the men's attitude toward work was a form of smugness. "In effect they say to me (and to the vast majority of white-collar workers): 'I do an honest day's work and you don't.'"[3]

More important, LeMasters claims, is that these men are not the strivers one expects to find in American society. They are not "struggling to get ahead, to rise in the social class structure." He reports that they seem to be "relatively content with their lot in this world." But then LeMasters adds, "Given their limited educational background, most of them feel that their *job is about as good as they could expect*"[4] (author's emphasis).

This last comment underscores the importance of the distinction between wishes and expectations. Several of the men reported ventures into businesses of their own, but either they failed at them, or the businesses interfered with their "independence and freedom." (As reported by LeMasters, these ventures without exception were in the secondary sector *and* in the free job market.)

In the conversations recorded by LeMasters, these working-class men do not seem to be as free of striving as he suggests. First of all, their comments are circumstance-bound expectations and do not express what they *wish*.

Second, the importance attached by the men to "independence and freedom" seems powerfully compensative. In the second chapter I stated that the religion of winning is composed of the two doctrines of individual freedom and equality of opportunity (or parity in competition). The importance of "independence and freedom" to the men clearly expresses the individual freedom doctrine.

The doctrine of equality of opportunity, with its stress on competition, is the aspect of the religion of winning that is dropped or compensated for in the work world by the men LeMasters studied. The reason is not that the work the blue-collar winners do is inferior. Anyone who has built something knows the creativity and satisfaction associated with construction. Rather, the point is that cultural pressures denigrate blue-collar work, no matter how creative and craftsmanlike it is. That the men LeMasters studied know this is reflected in the preoccupation with "independence and freedom." They protest too much.

Actually the men do not drop the desire to be on top. Rather the desire finds outlets in hunting, fishing, shooting pool, bowling, and owning a quality pickup truck. At the tavern a man's status did not depend on being a good pool player, but he had to excel at something like card playing, hunting, or drinking. To get respect, to receive deference from the group, he had to be better than just average in some pursuit. The only exception was a physically powerful man, who, LeMasters claims, "automatically enjoys high status unless he becomes an alcoholic or ruins his life in some fashion."[5]

The desire to get to the top is also expressed in the particular pride the men find in becoming intimate with another man's spouse or with a woman who "belongs" to another man. In such exploits the men do not seek sexual enjoyment only. Success in such sexual adventures assures their position in the tavern pecking order.[6]

On the basis of LeMasters's study, one might conclude that blue-collar winners are people who like their work, receive good pay and benefits, and find satisfaction in their work. The chief values of the men are "independence and freedom." Given their relative privilege, they attempt to organize their marriages, families, leisure, and energy around these values.

The Wives of the Blue-Collar Winners

What about the wives of these blue-collar winner men? What can be said about them and about their marriages to winner husbands?

LeMasters found considerable segregation of sex roles between the two. The men wanted their independence and freedom, and they wanted wives who would keep their home and children and not interfere with the husband and his ways. This attitude, of course, led to no little strain in many of the marriages, leading LeMasters to conclude that marriage was a better deal for a man than for a woman.

LeMasters also discovered a "difference in social class identification" between the wives and husbands. Most of the women had been gainfully employed outside the home at some point in their lives. However, only one of these women had held a blue-collar job. They typically were "cashiers, bookkeepers, clerks, telephone operators, typists, beauty operators—jobs which require the development of interpersonal skills with both sexes. In contrast, their husbands work in an all-male, one-sexed world and spend their days handling *things* rather than people."[7] The women therefore had greater exposure to middle-class norms than their husbands. Via TV and the mass media the women seemed exposed to a different socialization than the men. The latter love "the traditional world they grew up in whereas the women can see some advantages in the white-collar version of 'togetherness' in marriage."[8]

Yet these marriages had strengths. A blue-collar winner represents a "good catch" for these women, and these wives typically cannot afford to leave their husbands for trivial reasons. The husband's pay and benefits are good, and that means a great deal. Moreover, the people LeMasters studied came from traditional blue-collar backgrounds, so that the women were prepared to live with the kinds of men to whom they were married. Finally, both the men and women held negative attitudes about divorce and found little that was desirable about the divorced persons that frequented the tavern. This negative view of divorce was also sustained by the religious affiliations of the group: most of them were Roman Catholics or Lutherans. These religious views were stronger among the women than among the men.

Even though winner husbands and wives may like, even love, each other, they had serious reservations about the institution of marriage itself. Most of them felt that they married too soon and did not understand what they were getting into. Few of them realized the maturity that marriage required when they were first wed, and the battle of the sexes was a persistent dimension of their lives. An ongoing struggle persisted between the husband who wanted independence and freedom and the wife who sought deeper companionship in the marriage.

Not all marriages last, of course; some end in divorce and other marital failures become simply facade marriages. Perhaps the most important finding LeMasters made here was that one may not draw broad generalizations about the reasons for divorce and facade marriages. Indeed, the most striking thing about divorces and divorced people was the variety of reasons for divorcing. Some married too young; others hated the opposite sex; some felt unsuited for marriage; others had tried it and didn't like it; some had been jilted and abandoned; others had personality problems; for some divorce was the end of a long struggle with a spouse (for example, alcoholism); for others they simply chose the wrong person.[9]

Blue-collar winner husbands and their wives do not make up the whole membership of this life-style. A new group is emerging, made up of those women who work in jobs previously held by men. These are the blue-collar winner women.

Blue-Collar Winner Women

I mentioned earlier Mary Lindenstein Walshok's *Blue-Collar Women,* a study of successful working women in nontraditional blue-collar employment. Walshok called these women "pioneers," as indeed they are. Walshok's interest was to understand how they came to be pioneers. What were their working roots and roads to adulthood? How did they gain a sense of self as permanent members of the paid labor force? What were life at work and relationships at work like? And what is the meaning of nontraditional blue-collar work in their lives? These are some of the questions she sought to answer. Her findings provide a useful profile for blue-collar winner women.

Pioneers take risks. So Walshok began with the question what in their backgrounds gave these women the independence and capacity for risk taking? She found that their parents did not intentionally set out to make them into such independent people. "Rather, accidents of childhood, inadvertent granting of independence, family crises, and parental role models give rise to unexpected, unintended outcomes."[10] Walshok found that these women did not have "predictable, secure childhoods" in which they "could . . . count on constant care from parents" for female socialization. Yet they did obtain a sense of roots from their parents, usually their mothers. While they went through hard times growing up, things either "got better or were episodic rather than never-ending and uncontrollable." They knew the world was not an entirely predictable place, and they were required to be sufficiently independent to realize that they were not helpless. They had the kind of success models that demonstrated that "things can get better if you work at it."[11] In summary "the pioneer in the blue-collar world tends to be a woman who has come from a family background characterized by a subtle mix of emotional security, predictability, and trust in critical interpersonal relationships even though significant financial or family crises may be present." There can be security and hope, but security and happiness must be worked for.[12]

During adolescence these women continued to have "a great deal of personal independence." About half were only slightly involved in school cliques and school-related activities. They saw themselves as not especially attractive. They did not date and were not boy- and clothes-conscious the way so many girls were. Many were employed and spent their time outside school earning money. Some of them lived with boyfriends or husbands or were pregnant before completing school. "It was the rare woman who described a cheery, carefree adolescence full of school activities, parties, and boyfriends." These women had "a special kind of marginality and separateness that went beyond the predictable anxieties and loneliness tied to the transition into adulthood."[13]

By the time Walshok met the women of her study, they had a fairly clear understanding of the type of work they desired and expected that they would always work. "This sense of oneself as a permanent member of the paid labor force, with definite likes and dislikes for particular jobs and job settings" is what Wolshok calls the "stabilization of work role identity."[14] However, when these women first entered the work force, they did not know what they wanted to do. They wanted work that was interesting, challenging, and well paid, but mostly they knew what they did *not* want to do. What was different about them from most women was that they found out about jobs, and when opportunities came, they took advantage of them. They "opted out of the conventional track and tried unexplored territory."[15]

While these pioneers followed a variety of career paths, Walshok found that their "vocational interests and preferences evolved and became stabilized as a result of on-the-job experiences and employment opportunities. Specific interests and work commitments grew out of their employment experiences. . . ."[16] Here there is an important difference between blue-collar pioneers and middle-class and professional women. The latter develop interests and capacities apart from their work experience. They then seek out jobs in which they can express these interests and capacities. Most working-class women, in contrast, seem to develop their interests and capacities in the environs of the job itself. They increase their commitment and explore alternatives in the job setting rather than taking the direction of self-exploration and education, which is more characteristic of middle-class women.[17]

For example, a blue-collar woman develops skills as a welder's helper. She then uses this experience to take advantages of opportunities on the job to train and become a welder. In contrast, a middle-class elementary school teacher with an interest in psychology and counseling may use her summers to pursue a graduate degree and her weekends to take advantage of workshops and seminars.

Wolshok observes that the relationship between vocational preferences and vocational choices is "not a simple one-way matter, wherein attitudes and interests lead to specific choices. It varies by class, by race, and by other factors limiting the number of life-style alternatives available."[18] She challenges the stereotype of the employed, working-class woman that "focuses on her inconsistent work patterns, desire for sociable and nonchallenging work settings, and ability to do boring, routine work for long periods."[19] The women she studied had done such work but were not satisfied by it. Walshok wonders how many women workers who supposedly "prefer" and are "content with" routine, low-income jobs have simply surrendered to them because of the absence of other opportunities.[20]

Walshok found that these pioneer blue-collar women value the same thing in employment that men do. To be sure, full-time employment and a steady paycheck were the critical reasons for having jobs, but the jobs meant more than that. Five recurring themes were identified by Walshok and suggest the other values women sought in their work.

1. *Productivity*—both in terms of output of goods and services and in accomplishment.

2. *Challenge*—newness, variety, problem-solving opportunities and something unusual.

3. *Relatedness*—being in the swim of things, sociability, recognition, and feedback.

4. *Autonomy*—some control over the pace of work, discretion about the sequence and frequency of tasks.

5. *Well-being*—mental and physical satisfaction and "spillover" impact on self-identity and personal relationships.[21]

In order for the women to be successful pioneers Walshok found that both individual and situational characteristics were required. The woman most likely to succeed:

identifies herself as a worker from an early age;

is more task-oriented than interpersonally oriented;
is preoccupied with puzzles and problem solving;
gives nonideological interpretations to her own and others' (especially male) behavior;
has skills resulting from some advanced education;
knows how to seek out information and opportunities necessary for mastering tasks;
is in a network of competent, savvy peers;
receives support from friends and family for risk taking;
wants good compensation and benefits for her labor;
is secure about her employment prospects in skilled trades.[22]

Certain situational characteristics were also required for success:

. . . stable jobs;
. . . good compensation and benefits;
. . . effective mechanisms for employee representation;
. . . mechanisms that ensure a minimum level of familiarity with blue-collar work and workers prior to job assignment; [moreover, such situations]
focus on strategies for helping people become competent at particular jobs rather than striving for acceptance of newcomers in particular jobs;
spell out job requirements and expectations;
surround newcomers with competent and savvy men *and* women;
provide frequent feedback on performance.[23]

It should also be noted that most of these women were single or heads of a household. Only 25 percent of the women were married at the time of the study and only about 48 percent had children. This indicates which women were able to assume risks and give the time and commitment needed to be pioneers.[24]

In sum, then, what does it take for a woman to be a blue-collar winner? First, it takes pressure and intervention from government simply to open up jobs for women. Such opportunity does not come without the exercise of power. Second, it takes unique people, women with special family and adolescent backgrounds, who are socialized to run the risks and take advantage of the opportunities that come. Finally, it requires favorable situations—the kind of work settings in which women can learn on the job and develop their abilities, in which the pay and benefits are good, and so forth.

In other words, blue-collar winners are special women in special situations with opportunities made available by governmental power. That most people and most situations are not that special and that the exercise of governmental power remains ambiguous reinforce the general contrast between the religion of winning and the reality of losing.

In conclusion, blue-collar winners are those who have good pay and benefits and like their jobs. Typically they work in the primary sector of the economy and in contested and traditional job markets. They are supported by powerful unions or work in industries that provide commensurate pay and benefits as a way of keeping the unions out. Blue-collar winner men value "independence and freedom" and seek a life-style consistent with these values. Their wives, in contrast, tend to identify more with middle-class norms, a reflection, in part, of their own work experience, the impact of mass media, and other socialization. Blue-collar winner women are pioneers, a very special group of people both in terms of life experience and circumstances, who have been able to take advantage of governmental power and seek out jobs previously open almost exclusively to blue-collar winner men.

A final note, the future of blue-collar winners is uncertain. The de-skilling of work in the United States, the movement of American industry overseas, the shift from an industrial to a service-oriented society—all of these changes and more will have a fateful impact on all working-class people. The changes could reduce the number of blue-collar winners significantly by sharply cutting back on the proportion of good jobs with high pay in the United States. These changes are the most clear challenges to their "independence and freedom."

Blue-collar winners are a minority in the working-class world. Most blue-collar people either do not have high wages or do not enjoy their work or both. Among these are the blue-collar respectables, who are discussed in the next chapter.

5

Blue-Collar Respectables

In the sixth grade I came home from school with a "U" (for unsatisfactory) in deportment on my report card. My mother looked at it sternly and "cleared up" the issue with haste. "Look, boy. I don't care whether you're dumb or smart; I love you anyhow. But you don't have to be smart to be good! Now, the next time you come home with a report card showing you flunked conduct, I'm going to tear up your ['existential ground of being' expressed in primitive Anglo-Saxon language]!"

Then she added, "This is a respectable family. We work hard for it, and we damned well expect to keep it that way." It took me twenty years to understand how important my mother's comment was.

Respectability takes hard work. It means struggling with the bills month to month, paying a little more on this account one month and a little more on another the next. It means trying to "be clean" and to "live in a decent place." It means being able to hold your head up when you are around other people "downtown" or "in the neighborhood" or "up at the school."

Respectability places a high premium on *order*. The reason

is that the family has to live carefully in order to stay above water. If a big enough setback occurs—it does not have to be major—indebtedness will overwhelm the resources of the family. The tension that results brings on fights, resentment, and estrangement.

Order is a prerequisite of respectability. When the one goes, so does the other. This is a basic reason why respectable people want the family, the school, and the church to be mutually supportive. They want the reinforcement, the support, the help to keep things together. It is an understandable desire.

The impulses of respectability come from a deep human wish for self-respect, and there are many injuries of class that take away self-respect. In our society self-respect depends to a great extent on achievement, self-capacity (culturally recognized), and class. Even the young—the fortunate young—among working-class youth who go to college

> are made to feel inadequate by a "laying-on of culture" practiced in college by their teachers and the more privileged students—a process that causes people to feel inadequate in the same way "status incongruity" does, by subjecting them to an unfamiliar set of rules in a game where respect is the prize.[1]

Perhaps it is because self-respect is so closely related to class that respectability is not culturally the "real" thing. Respectability is second-best, a hand-me-down, and, hence, compensative; that is, it is an attempt to make up for what one did not get. It is like being the "best sport" in a contest instead of being the winner. If one cannot be a big success, a big shot, one can *at least* be respectable.

When one violates blue-collar people's respectability, one is spitting on something sacred. It is sacred because it is gained at such a high cost (the loss of winner status) and is known by its bearers to be second rate. That's why the rage is so vehement when someone transgresses the canons of respectability in a neighborhood, school, or church.

I have seen pastors go into blue-collar churches and communities, advancing life-styles, especially with the young people, that challenged the relationships of the home, church, and school. They could not fathom why they incurred such wrath from their congregations. The reaction demonstrated for them once again that the people were "unenlightened" and simply "unwilling to deal with change." Usually these pastors then sought out congregations of professional and business people that were open and able to take advantage of the enormous "talents" of these pastors.

An insensitive misuse of people occurs when helping professionals denigrate life-styles they do not understand, especially when the life-styles have been bought at such a high price. To be sure, the objection can be made that these life-styles work against the very people who pay the price; in other words, respectability prevents people from developing ideologies and organizations to call into question the circumstances of their lives.

The point is, however, that such change will not begin unless the change agent shows an appreciation for a respectable life-style and what it means to its loyal devotees. When professionals reduce life-styles to wrongheadedness or stupidity or "disfunctional" values, they miss the deprivations and constraints with which many families contend and forget the hunger people have for dignity and self-respect.

In social-science literature this respectability life-style is usually associated with the lower-middle class, but it is very much a part of the lives of many blue-collar people. That respectability is a blue-collar life-style is borne out by the work of Joseph T. Howell in his book *Hard Living on Clay Street.* What I call "respectability," he refers to as "settled living."

Howell sees the settled-living families he studied resembling the typical blue-collar family. They are usually "church-going, teetotaling, politically and socially conservative." They have stable marriages and own their own homes. Territorially rooted in the community, they tend to belong to a variety of local groups. More cautious and refined, these settled-living people are concerned about how other people view them. They are more protective of their children, whom they strictly discipline, and many of their children go to college.[2] Howell observes that these are the "respectable" members of the blue-collar neighborhood he studied in metropolitan Washington, D.C.

Blue-collar respectability is easily recognized in working-class neighborhoods. The respectability families have small, neat homes that reflect the intensive care of their owners. The grass is cut; the flowers and gardens are—if anything—given too much attention. The houses are carefully painted and often are surrounded by a chain-link fence.

The homes are important for many reasons. Usually the house is the major holding of wealth the family has. Bought through the F.H.A. and paid for with struggle in the early years of marriage, a house is one of the basic ways for a blue-collar family to claim that it has "made it." Owning one's own home and the way one takes care of it are forms of status. They enable a family to set itself apart from the "white trash" and, often, "the niggers" who may be moving into white working-class areas. For black families, owning one's home and taking care of it are ways to proclaim "We are *not* niggers, and we are as worthy as anyone."

The house is basic to one's stake in the neighborhood. The investment in the house places one's destiny in the neighborhood. On this basis the neighborhood becomes the center of meaning and value. Often members of one's extended family live nearby. Hence, one's wealth, status, kinship, meaning, and destiny can be bound up with the house and its neighborhood.

One's home, of course, is important to almost all persons, but it holds special meaning for respectables. Sennett and Cobb report on Ricca Kartides, a first-generation immigrant from Greece to Boston. Kartides is an educated person who, in migrating to the United States, got trapped into manual labor, working as a janitor. In the United States Kartides has not found reciprocal respect across class boundaries. The United States lacks the rituals by which people might transcend class lines. When he first worked as a maintenance man in the apartment complex where he also lived, he was ordered to use the back door at all times and not to allow his children to play on the lawn that surrounded the building.

Kartides responded to this indignity "by making heroic efforts of time, work, and personal sacrifice so that he could own a home of his own." The home was his sanctuary, the place where his position in society would not be thrown up to him. Inside the home was the space to be free, "and what I mean by freedom is my children can play without nobody telling them what to do."[3]

Yet this quest for sanctuary came at a high price. Kartides worked fourteen hours a day at two jobs to pay for the house. He sacrificed his social life and had little time to enjoy the very thing for which he paid so dearly.

He knows he is trapped. He knows he has not gotten the rewards he wants. Yet he was not willing to be just "Ricca the janitor," going through the back door and shouting his kids off the apartment lawn. He could not bear it. "So it was not because I wanted to make too much money; it was because I wanted to buy things, things I like, to live decently. . . ."[4]

The home is not only a haven and a rampart of decency; it can also be the object of one's creative powers. Lillian Rubin points out that home projects may be compensative for one's job. Men who work at dull, routine jobs and who find few personal satisfactions and precious little sense of mastery may find home projects valuable. These home projects may be the one way in which they can exercise the full range of skills and competencies they possess and utilize their own judgment and initiative.[5]

However, women may have much more ambivalence about the house. On the one hand, if a woman works outside the home, her time at home may be absorbed with the cleaning and chores of maintaining a house and family. While she may take great pride in her home, it is also the place where she works a second full-time job. On the other hand, if she is a homemaker, her greatest wish for her leisure time may be to go out, while her husband may want to stay home and work on pet projects. As Rubin says: "For him the house is a haven; for her, a prison."[6] It is a prison in which she takes enormous pride, but it can be a prison nonetheless.

Conventional Morality

Working-class people, in general, profess devotion to a conventional morality, but the ones most deeply committed to it are the respectables. For them conventional morality is an expression of and the narrow path to decency. Deviation from that path and moral failure lead to degradation and the loss of the vital ingredient that separates them from the "no-goods," "the ne'er-do-wells," and "the white trash," and cost them their claim to station with those above them: the respectability which may be second rate to achievement but is a claim to moral superiority.

The ingredients of conventional morality are many, and they read like the hand-me-downs of the history of the American character. It is a morality of restraint, of discipline, and of hard work. Some would call it a morality of repression, which is probably true, but the people who voice that judgment do not seem to care about the people they describe.

Conventional morality means being straight. Being straight means not engaging in questionable activities: wild parties, heavy drinking or maybe drinking at all, and relating to certain kinds of people with bad reputations, and so on. It also means to be trustworthy. One's word is as good as one's bond. "If I tell you I'll do something, you can count on it."

There is a strong sense that a person reaps what he or she sows—if not immediately, then in the long run. This is reflected from time to time in country music. The wailful song done by Hank Williams is a significant testimony to this precept of conventional morality:

> Your Cheatin' Heart will make you weep
> You'll cry and cry and try to sleep
> But sleep won't come the whole night through
> Your Cheatin' Heart will tell on you.[7]

Powerful restraints operate in sexual morality. Preachments against promiscuity abound. Daughters are urged to remain virgins until they marry, and sons are repeatedly taught to be nice boys. One's sexuality, like everything else, must be kept under control. Sex is powerful, and its capacity for upsetting the cart of respectability is real. It can destroy the stability of the family, disrupt the coalition with church and school, and dirty a reputation so doggedly achieved.

"Permissiveness" is a dirty word for most blue collarites.

Respectables take pride in the strict disciplining of their children. Discipline is seen as a fundamental expression of parental care. Moreover, respectable families are usually child-centered. Parents sacrifice themselves for their children in order to provide them with opportunities to get ahead, "to have the chance" they did not have. These parents do not see themselves being oppressive to their children; they just do not want to spoil them. They want to prepare them to live in the world they know. A good many upper middle-class professionals chortle at this attitude and approach. But with their money and position these professionals can "afford" permissiveness. They are reminiscent of Mark Twain's view of a Christian gentleman: a poker player with five aces.

Conventional morality stands in sharp contrast to the situational morality of business and professional people. In their jobs they have to make many decisions. These decisions entail many options, and these must be carefully weighed and balanced. Business and professional decisions, therefore, must take situational variables carefully into account. Blue-collar work does not often entail these kinds of decisions. Blue-collar people work under instructions. Their job is to do it *right*.

One day in the oil field we were laying a pipeline through a swamp and I, new at the job, was trying to stab a joint of pipe into the collar of another pipe. Since the pipe was twenty feet long and weighed two hundred pounds, it was not easy to do. I was obviously inept and struggling when Snooks Britt yelled out at me, "Hey, college boy, this ain't like it is in school. You can't do it any way you want to. And yore opinion don't mean a damned thing. There's a right way, and all the other ways are wrong. If you don't do it right, you can't do it." Conventional morality grows, in part at least, from this kind of experience and is fueled by the constraints and deprivations of the blue-collar world.

Conventional morality is a morality of realism and conformity because it knows how tough the world is, especially when one wants to please. Maintaining balance in a world of financial obligations, requirements of decency, and the canons of being a nice person is not the basis for an expansive ethic.

A close friend of mine named Tommy told me this story of his youth. His twenty-eight-year-old sister, an alcoholic who was violent when she got drunk, came home and made a vicious scene. Sixteen-year-old Tommy had to help his mother and aunt subdue her amidst the worst shelling of verbal obscenities he had ever experienced. Struggling to avoid repeated efforts by his sister to kick him in the groin, he bear-hugged her and carried her to a bed. While he held her, his mother and aunt tied her to the bed.

Tommy broke down into tears. His eyes red and his face splotched from crying, he had fifteen minutes to get himself "straightened out" before his friends came by to pick him up and go to a party.

My mother told me it was okay. She told me to put cold water on my face, that I would look all right in a little while. "Hold your head up, Son, you're as good as anybody. Don't let this bother you. We have to face these things with a smile, even when they hurt."

I didn't see how I could go to the party. I didn't want to. My Mother didn't tell me I had to go. I just knew that if I didn't, people would wonder why and I wouldn't be able to explain.

So I got a cold towel, and when my friends came by, I was standing on the street, smiling and ready to go. They didn't seem to notice anything, and I never told them.

Alienation

Conforming without achieving the promised rewards exacts its price. Hard work and living "close to the line" give life a ragged edge, a sense of dissatisfaction and incompleteness.

Blue-collar respectables are the conformists, the ones who have bought into the system. They believe in hard work, and they believe the religion of winning: that anyone can make it to the top if he or she has the determination and the brains. When they do not succeed, what consolation can they give themselves? God knows they tried, that they had the determination. On what, then, can they blame their failure but their own brains or the incapacity of their brains? Can anything be more devastating for one's self-image?

No one can live with such a self-image without relief and

escape from time to time. Mostly, however, blue-collar respectables contend with damage to their personal dignity by stifling
their anger and pain and by redefining success so that it is
more commensurate with their modest achievements. Sometimes they compensate for the assaults through the accumu-
lation of home, furniture, and "nice things." It's easy to make
fun of an overdone house with its twelve-by-fifteen-foot living
room filled with French provincial furniture covered with clear
plastic and drapes that belong in a palace. It's easy until one
sees the struggle and the pain behind the decorating. Yet often,
even these possessions do not work. Then come explosions of
anger and sometimes deep withdrawals into oneself.[8]

Alienation can also lead to deep resentment. If one is a
conformist and does believe in the American dream and sub-
stitutes respectability for the real thing, who then does one
blame when success does not come? At the deepest level, as we
have seen, one blames one's self, but not only one's self.

Such persons know they are not getting their fair share. In
his study, Howell found that "they thought the cause for the
problems had to do with blacks and white liberals." The settled-
living people, as Howell calls them, have a stake in the society,
and they feared that what they had was being taken away "by
liberal elitists and given to the poor, the blacks, and the 'lazy
bums on welfare.'"[9]

These settled-living people were very conservative, Howell
found. Although they tended to vote Republican, they felt the
Republicans were really too liberal but were the lesser of two
evils. Some spoke appreciatively of George Wallace as a pres-
idential candidate in the '68 election, but did not vote for him
because he "didn't have a chance of winning."[10] The ministers
of the area described their congregations as "very, very conservative."[11] The settled-living people were the most active
people in the community politically, and they were the most
conservative.

A few of the people were extremely right wing. They tended
to see people and events they disapproved of as parts of a
communist conspiracy. They saw people like Nicholas von Hoff-
man as communists and pornography, sex education, the peace

movement, and hard rock music as strategic efforts by the communist conspiracy to bring America down.

Changes in the Meaning of Respectability

People with respectability life-styles have undergone rough times recently because of shifts occurring in American culture. Daniel Yankelovich reports that "familial success" was the dominant goal of life in the United States up until the early seventies. "More than in any other domain of psychoculture, changes in the meaning of familial success are reshaping our rules of living."[12] While most Americans still define their life goals in relation to familial success and a minority continue to accept it without change, the vast majority only partly subscribe to it, changing one or more of its basic themes.

Yankelovich's definition of familial success is in one way very close to my use of the term respectability. He contends that the concept has "three sets of shared meanings: the intactness and well-being of the family; enough money to provide some of the luxuries of life as well as security; and a hankering after respectability and acceptance."[13]

The basic difference between Yankelovich's view of respectability and my own is that he does not deal explicitly with its compensative nature. He sees respectability drawing its deep roots from the

need to belong, surely one of the most potent of all human drives. ... To be human is to belong, to be part of an entity larger than oneself—a family, a tribe, a neighborhood, a religion, an ethnic group, a social class, a profession, a society, a civilization. ... A respectability badge is a sign of belonging.[14]

I have no quarrel with this view except to say that respectability as a direct outgrowth of the need to belong is in deep conflict with the value of winning in an achievement culture. The value of winning, in terms of what is *wanted,* often supersedes the impulse to respectability. In terms of what people must settle for, however, respectability is the dominant lifestyle practiced. Viewed this way, Yankelovich might agree that respectability is powerfully compensative.

He sees one of the main sources of confusion about success in America in the overlapping meaning of respectability and "social mobility"—the latter being close to what I call the religion of winning. While respectability can be shared by all, social mobility is more limited. "There are no inherent limits to the number of respectability badges a society can create, and no basis for limiting them to a select class or group." However, "social mobility is another matter. By definition, it is limited. The search for higher status takes place in a hierarchical world."[15]

Why is respectability changing? Yankelovich reports several findings that are important for our purposes here. The first reason is because respectability is constituted, in part, of a self-denial ethic that is presently challenged by a self-fulfillment ethic gaining strength in the United States. As I have shown, respectability requires sacrifice. Often parents live and work for their children and to gain respect, as did Kartides the janitor. Yankelovich argues that the affluence the United States enjoyed from the end of World War II until the early seventies brought with it an ethic of self-fulfillment. People—especially the young and college educated—came to believe that they had a duty to self and that life was supposed to be intrinsically satisfying and to offer expansive opportunities in which to express oneself. This ethic of self-fulfillment emphasizes individualism rather than belonging. It emphasizes the inner person. Hence "the shared meaning of respectability diminishes, and belongingness loses ground to individualism."[16]

Second, this development was accompanied by significant changes in social norms that shifted toward looser, freer codes of behavior. These have affected marriage, family, sex, and children. While there seems to be a greater toleration of difference, there is a growing distrust of basic institutions. These changes are eroding the meaning of respectability.[17]

Imagine, for example, how blue-collar respectable parents deal with the fact of having a son or daughter living with someone without being married. What do they say to the neighbors when the couple comes to visit? How do the parents describe the young couple's relationship or—perhaps more typical—how do they avoid describing it? Yankelovich points out that the respectability badges are disappearing. "Having a family without a record of divorce, maintaining a well-kept home, exhibiting one's children as well-mannered and neat and clean in appearance have all been drained of much of their symbolic significance." As a result, it becomes more difficult to prove to oneself or to others that one is respectable.[18]

This is precisely what many blue-collar people protest when they claim that somebody changed the rules of the game. Listen to one acquaintance of mine.

> Look, I did it by the book, the American way. When they said, "Go, fight," I went. When they said, "Work," I busted my tail. When they said, "Raise a decent family," I loved my wife and taught my kids right from wrong. But it don't mean a damned thing anymore. People think you're crazy to play by the rules. I'll tell you it's a . . . mess!

The point here is not that blue-collar people have abandoned respectability. As Yankelovich reports, they are among the most conservative people culturally. Moreover, "the working-class American more often hesitates to risk abandoning a familiar path for one that poses hidden dangers, an attitude that comes at least partly from reality-testing associated with social class." Blue-collar people do not share "the self-confident conviction that the world will cooperate with one's plans . . . because their own and their family experience suggests the opposite, namely that the world does not usually cooperate. Therefore, 'Why take a chance?'"[19]

The result is confusion. Working-class people still hold to respectability; yet they do so with an intense awareness that someone or something has changed the rules of the game. They are also influenced by the ethic of self-fulfillment. However, for them self-fulfillment does not become a life-style, but a cherished—often small—aspect of their life-style. It often appears as a hobby or other leisure-time pursuit. One woman goes to the beauty parlor every week. "I owe it to myself. When I was growing up, my hair was always a mess. I'll tell you, even if I have to give up eating one day a week, I'm going to the beauty shop." It happens with any number of men in athletic leagues. One softball player said, "Listen, this is all I ever wanted to do. I'd rather play ball than do anything in the world. The job may be lousy, but if I can get out here two or three nights a week, I can make it." For many grown men, playing a boy's game is the major expression of their search for self-fulfillment.

Finally, Yankelovich observes that the self-fulfillment ethic and its challenge to the familial success model emerged during a period of unparalleled affluence in United States society. This affluence is now under assault from inflation, unemployment, the rising cost of energy, and the declining productivity of American industry. With this assault the spirit of optimism in the United States has turned to one of apprehension. Among the first to be hit by these economic reversals are blue-collar Americans.

Blue-Collar Winners and Respectables

In conclusion, a distinction needs to be made between blue-collar winners and respectables. While winners may value respectability highly—some of them certainly do—they have the kind of work satisfaction, income, and fringe benefits that make them less in need of the compensative support of respectability. If you will, they can tell the world to "stick it." They possess skills and knowledge that have not, as yet, been reduced to the efficiencies of the assembly line and production procedures.

Support for this view is found in LeMasters's work on blue-collar artistocrats. Their life-style maximizes independence and freedom. Respectable blue-collar people, however, are too conformist in their orientation to place as much value on independence and freedom. Theirs is a life-style more concerned with measuring up and trying to please people. Moreover, they are closer to the line of survival. They struggle more. There is more to keep in balance.

When people realize or become convinced that the juggling act is not worth the price and when they have given up on respectability, they struggle mainly to "get by." These are the blue-collar survivors, and we turn next to them.

6

Blue-Collar Survivors

There are several basic differences between blue-collar survivors and blue-collar winners and respectables. First, while blue-collar survivors may—usually they do not—make good money, their jobs are dull, routine, and monotonous. For this reason they do not have the satisfaction in their work that characterized the people in LeMasters's study of blue-collar aristocrats. Their lives are, therefore, subject to the impact of problems entailed by such jobs.

Second, they are more typically in jobs that pay so little that life is an ongoing financial struggle. While they hope to get ahead, mainly they just "get by."[1] Found mainly in semi-skilled work, these people are not likely to see their situation changed in any fundamental way. Some pay increases and advantages come with seniority, but in the range of jobs generally available, these are not large. Hence, where one is at twenty-eight is very similar to where one will be when forty or fifty.

Third, blue-collar survivors do not buy into respectability. It just does not seem worth the trouble. Not greatly concerned about personal reputation, they anticipate a lifetime of staying pretty much in the same job or moving through a series of similar ones. They do not have many illusions about who they are and what the job is. Theirs are anonymous jobs for anonymous people. Survivors do not have to "sell themselves" or rely upon family background or display consumption skills; fundamentally, they simply have to be willing to work. The work itself, being dull and deadening, requires adjustment, working while keeping one's mind off the work, and finally brings resignation, giving up hopes for future advancement. The latter is something hard to do, as I shall show.

Kahl contends that the basic fact about semi-skilled working-class life is that it is on a flat level. The responsibilities of the jobs, the pay, the benefits do not vary much. So there is no reason to be ambitious or to work hard when there is really no place to go.[2]

I know a man named Bob who is in his late thirties. He has worked at an auto assembly plant for *nine* years. For him there is no place to go. I once asked him if he liked it.

"The money's good. I can't make as much money doin' anything else. I'd like to get on days so I didn't have to work nights. Working nights screws things up. I don't think I'll ever get used to working nights and sleeping days. I don't know, it just doesn't seem, uh, natural, you know what I mean? But I'll have to get more seniority before I can bump anybody out there and get on days."

The automakers I know talk about the plant as "out there" or "out at Ford." "Out there" seems to be a place separate, set apart from the rest of their lives, not really connected to much else. It seems that they must move out of life to go to that necessary place (work). "Out there" for the auto-worker men is the place where they have to go and "get it done." They will do it; they will endure and survive.

"What do you do out there?" I asked.

"Oh, I paint cars. You ever been out there?"

"Yeah, I saw the place where they paint. You have to be pretty good to do that, don't you?"

"Aw, it takes a little while to get the knack of it, but it ain't too hard. The main thing is holding that paint gun all day. That's the hard part. You just don't realize how heavy that gun can get after a while. I try to get my mind off of it and think about other things. You know, think about what I'm gonna do that night, think about ball games. You know, just think about anything. [Pause] I've been painting out there now for nine years. Sometimes I just wonder how much longer I can hold onto that spray gun. [Pause] But, you know, you just can't start thinking like that. It just makes things worse. You just gotta keep your mind off of it."

On the basis of her research Lillian Rubin reports that most blue-collar men work at jobs that provide little opportunity for utilization of skill or independent judgment or for expression of freedom and autonomy. Consequently the jobs have few intrinsic rewards and provide little status in the workplace or outside it. A worker finds scarce opportunity for seeing oneself as a good man or woman. These people get through the day by doing their jobs "and numbing themselves to the painful feelings of discontent— trying hard to avoid the question, 'Is this what life is all about?'"[3]

Blue-collar survivors do not really fit into the stereotype of hating to work. They do not disparage work per se. They often hate their jobs—and for good reason—but that is quite different from hating work. One study did a test of the commitment of people to work. It looked at the behavior of people who had won the lottery in New York and New Jersey. The lottery winners were thoroughly committed to work, but not to their jobs. When the economic necessity of a job ended, these people continued to work but found new jobs.[4]

Survivor women are a breed apart from the winners studied by Walshok. Many of them would be delighted to stay home from the jobs they hold but not because home is so great. As I have shown, many women prefer to work at jobs that are dull and monotonous rather than face the deadening reality of housework. Not women survivors. To be sure, they like to get out of the house, and they do not care for the mundane and demeaning character of housework, and they like to have money of their own to spend. But being home is just preferable to the kind of work they do. This is especially true when time at home becomes a second eight-hour job. The problem for most survivor women is that they do not have a choice.

As with most women with families the survivor is caught in the multiple roles of worker, wife, and mother. She does not work for "pin money." While her salary is usually considerably below that of her husband, her income is nevertheless necessary to the family economic balance. She

> faces continuing limitations. She will be a temporary worker; she will have a high absenteeism rate; she will change jobs frequently—or so her potential employers assume. While none of these assumptions remains valid, they are among the forces keeping women in low-level positions.[5]

Her jobs will be overwhelmingly in the secondary sector of the economy and in the free market. When not in these, she is caught in the internal labor market seemingly designed for women and ethnic minorities.

As a wife and mother, she is torn by the demands of husband and children which she must balance while being a housekeeper. The children demand her attention; her husband wants her to be feminine, and the clothes need to be washed, the house cleaned, and the dishes put away. Her work outside the home creates other pressures. Most men do not want their spouses to work, and because it is necessary, they feel diminished. The men see it as some failing of their own, and the women find themselves trying to salve their spouses' egos while recognizing the necessity of their employment.

> My husband says I don't have to work, but if I don't, we'll never get anywhere. I guess it's a matter of pride with him. It makes him feel bad, like he's not supporting us good enough. I understand how he feels, but I also know that, no matter what he says, if I stop working, when the taxes on the house have to be paid, there wouldn't be any money if we didn't have my salary.[6]

Obviously, not all survivor women are married. "Desertion, illegitimacy, divorce, separation, and widowhood have increased dramatically [since World War II], making many women into breadwinners of some sort." Roughly 40 percent of the families living in poverty are headed by women.[7] The survivor woman who heads her own family is then usually up against even greater odds than one with a husband. Her struggle to make ends meet takes on heroic proportions. Getting by becomes a monumental achievement.

These women start their days early. They leave the children with relatives or at a day-care center or get them off to school. Their jobs are among the most tedious, typically requiring speed and dexterity. When the job is over, they rush home to make sure the children made out all right. Then it is time to cook supper, do what they can with the pains and the joys of the children's day, look for time of their own, restore some semblance of order to the house or apartment, and collapse.

They anticipate no great change in their future except to manage to raise their children and make it through the week. Respectability for these survivor women is a luxury they cannot afford. It is enough if they can pay the bills and get the kids raised. Their jobs are dead end. They know that. Most of them hope they will meet a man—a decent one this time, one not so dumb (meaning that he won't chase other women, drink so much, or move from one job to another) and get married. Finding the time and the place to meet a man is another story, and for many of them, finally, it is as unrealistic as becoming rich or finding gold in the dishwater.

Separation of Life and Work

Because of the nature of their work, blue-collar survivors attempt to separate work from the rest of life, an effort that does not often succeed. Some men, for example, develop home projects or special hobbies as compensation for the deadening work they do. Yet, these become the occasion for retreating from the family. The projects can be a way of being at home without being present.[8]

For others life at home is a continuation of the experience of work.

Unfortunately, true creativity is rare, for the men carry over into leisure activities the attitudes they have so deeply absorbed on the job, attitudes of passivity that demand something to do to pass the time. A man cannot get full satisfaction from hobby activities when he realizes that work is at the center of one's life and all else is, for Americans, peripheral. . . .[9]

The thing we so often misunderstand is that a job affects a person much more than a person affects a job. This notion flies in the face of what many Americans believe, but research bears it out. I had occasion earlier to report the work of Kohn and Schooler and their findings of the key role self-direction plays in life:

> occupational self-direction has the most potent and most widespread effects of all the occupational conditions we have examined. In terms of psychological effects, the central fact of occupational life today . . . is the opportunity to use initiative, thought, and independent judgment in one's work—to direct one's own occupational activities.[10]

Moreover, Kohn and Schooler found that the attitude that one has at work is likely to be the same when not working. That is, a man with a dull, routine, monotonous job will very likely pursue leisure in the same unimaginative way. They state, "Nowhere in these data is there evidence that men turn their occupational frustrations loose on the nonoccupational world or try to find compensation in nonoccupational realities for occupational lacks and grievances."[11] Dull work leads people to pursue dull lives.[12] Creative, imaginative work influences people to seek richer experience when not working. Albert Camus wrote: "Without work all life goes rotten. But when work is soulless, life stifles and dies."[13]

Meanwhile, the women go from the monotony of the job to unending chores at home. Even if the men moonlight and pick up extra work, it is still highly doubtful that they put in the hours women do. Busy with supper and the kids and preparing for the next day, the survivors usually find themselves able to relax in front of the TV toward the end of the evening. This is just before going to sleep and getting up to do it all over again the next day. One acquaintance of mine said, "I'll tell you, there just ain't time to do anything for yourself anymore. By the time I get supper over, help the young-uns with their school work and God knows what else, it's time to fix our lunches for the next day, throw in a load of clothes, and then sit down to fall asleep in front of TV. One day just seems to look like the next."

Hope and Dreams

Blue-collar survivors do have dreams, but the realization of dreams seem to evade them, at least the great majority of them. For many the dream is "to get ahead," to pay up the bills, and to set aside a nest egg, to prepare for a rainy day.

For some that comes, at least temporarily, when the children have left home. Perhaps by then they have paid off the house and have "a little extra." This is short-lived, however, because retirement makes things close again.

Others hope to own their own businesses. One twenty-three-year-old auto worker I know had dreams of opening his own store. He and his wife had bought a piece of land near a large lake development.

"We've got a nice place there. You know, it's not much. The house is okay, nothing fancy. We've got three acres. There's a small building right on the road that I could turn into a store. I've been thinking about a bait-and-tackle shop. We can't do it right away, but I'd like to do it someday. Right now I need the work at Claycomo [the community where the Ford plant is]. But I don't want to spend my whole life out there. I'd like a little business of my own."

This dream of owning a small business, which once was "the standard aspiration of middle-class sons," has become "an escape myth for factory workers, and the chances of succeeding in such a business are low; for relatively few of those who manage to get started can stay in business very long."[14] In Chinoy's study of autoworkers, seventeen out of sixty-two workers had seriously planned to leave the factory. After four years only six had done so. Of these three had made it: one was a college student; the second became a policeman; and the third opened his own tool-and-die shop. The other three did not do so well: one switched to a job in which he was doing about the same thing, the second left the factory only to return a short time later, and the third left the factory, but could not be traced by Chinoy.[15]

By the time that workers are in their forties, they accept the idea that the factory is their future. Like inmates in a prison, they have seen few "go over the wall." They realize full well that few of these courageous or desperate souls make the change. Dreams of escaping the factory are lost in the realities of steady income, seniority, fringe benefits, and a dependable pension. Knowing that their families depend on them, they accommodate themselves to the job and the routine by not thinking about the work, by doing it automatically. The job is something they just have to do; the less involved with it they are personally, the easier it is to live with. Life's satisfactions come from events and relationships away from the factory: their families, homes, vacations, and hopes for their children's success. To the new worker breaking into the job, they give the advice they've learned from the intimacy that only years of experience can bring, "You get used to it."

In conclusion, blue-collar survivors do not typically have the pay, the benefits, or the job satisfaction of blue-collar winners. If they do work in the primary sector and receive good pay, they are in the most deadening jobs. They have no truck with respectability because it exacts too high a price. It is not worth it. What leisure time they have seems little more satisfying than their jobs. In fact, some studies report that the job experience determines their leisure-time pursuits more than any other factor. For survivors, life is a process of building callouses for body and soul so that one can make it through the day and the night, so that one can get by.

For only one other blue-collar group is life more struggle. This group is hard-living working people. They are the subject of the next chapter.

7

Blue-Collar Hard Living

I grew up with a boy named Jack. He was big, tall, and fast. When we were in the eighth grade, a teacher, named "Miss Lovett," came to our school from Mississippi State College for Women. She was the first *really* attractive teacher we ever had, and we boys would do anything for her—except memorize poems.

One day she had us memorize "To a Daffodil." Scott Byrd, later to distinguish his literary powers with a Ph.D. in English literature, got up and ripped it. (We hated him when he did that so easily.) Then Jack got up. He had on "floodbritches"— six inches up from the floor—and his shirts never did fit. His clothes had a way of looking uncomfortable on him, as if they were stretched beyond reasonable doubt. When he stood, his elbows always stuck out.

"Miss Lovett, I didn't learn no po'm."

"Poem, Jack."

"Yes'm, po'm."

"Why didn't you learn the poem?"

"Aw, Miss Lovett, I can't learn no po'm."

"Any poem."

"Yes'm . . . I'll tell you what, Miss Lovett. I'll learn that po'm if you'll answer *yes* to one question. Miss Lovett, when I qui-tuate from school and go out there in the oil field to get me a job, is that tool pusher who runs the rig going to say to me, 'Recite me a po'm?'"

Miss Lovett left the room. I am convinced that she went to get the book on the philosophy of education.

Jack became an all-state football player, fell in love, and married the daughter of a well-to-do family. They had a child and split shortly thereafter. There was no way that Jack could provide the life to which she had grown accustomed.

Jack did, in fact, graduate and he then went to the oil field. There he "slung steel," muscled up to 225 pounds (big in those days). Except for a cushion of beer blubber on his stomach, he was rock-hard. On Friday and Saturday nights he'd go to the High Hat Club, a county-line beer joint that my father told me not ever to enter unless I "had a pistol on each hip and was prepared to use 'em or eat 'em." Jack would belly up to the bar, swallow down a six-pack or two, and then yell, "It's house cleanin' time!" With that he began to knock people down and throw them through plate-glass windows. It once took eight deputies to arrest him.

That's hard living.

The connection between Jack's life-style and achievement religion may seem distant, but they connect intimately. Jack is still trying to be a winner. In his world there is no difference between being the toughest man at the High Hat and being a doctor or lawyer or such. Yet there is all the difference in the world, and Jack knows it, which is one reason he drinks so much.

In popular terminology the people who are into hard living are "the losers." Typically, they are blue collarites who are poor or near-poor. They are not striving for success, at least not in conventional ways. They gave up on that long ago.

Joseph T. Howell in his study of a working-class suburb of Washington, D.C., has suggested that hard living is an "in-tense, episodic, and uninhibited" approach to life. Hard living emphasizes individualism, calling a person to be true to oneself, and typically this is done at tremendous cost to oneself. While it would be simplistic to say that hard-living people are not concerned about the future, they are "pre-occupied with the problems and drama of day-to-day life, particularly personal relationships."[1]

In his study Howell provides seven general characteristics of hard living. I shall report his findings in some detail.

1. *Heavy drinking.* Drinking is a way of life. One of the people in the neighborhood where Howell lived and did his study claimed that when it came to drinking, there were three kinds of people on Clay Street: "Them that don't drink, them that drink a lot, them that drink a . . . lot."[2] The majority of people Howell knew fell into the middle category. Alcohol was a part of their daily life; they often drank a six-pack of beer and a pint of whiskey every evening.

The third group were "conspicuously drunk most of the time." As a result of the inability to control their drinking, alcohol had played an important part in the "disintegration of their personal lives" and they were looked down on in the neighborhood as "drunks."[3]

Binges were a distinct pattern of drinking on Clay Street. Some people went on a binge every weekend, but most did it less frequently. A binge could last several weeks. As one might guess, these binges were the cause, or at least the occasion of much of the violence and conflict in the neighborhood. Domestic quarrels and fights usually occurred during drinking bouts. Men would shoot up their apartments and—from time to time— other people and themselves.

When asked *why* people drank, the answers were varied. Some described it simply as "stupid," something people did who knew no better. Another answered, "Man takes a drink to ease his mind. To ease the tension." With many of the men, drinking was associated with "strength, virility, and toughness." Drinking was also a way to escape from problems, a means of coping. One woman said, "My bottle *is* my tranquilizer. . . . If I didn't have it, I don't think I could make it through the day."[4] For others it was one way to get "the most out of life, of having fun." Alcohol helped to bring excitement and fun to a life that was otherwise hard. Howell reports there was less talk about *why* people went on binges. They seemed to be something that people just did. The excesses of violence and conflict were explained as something that just "happens when you're drunk."[5]

2. *Marital instability.* Howell observes that "practically everyone he knew on Clay Street had been married before." Many marriages were shaky, and a great deal of "time, emotion, and energy" was spent on marital relationships. These marriages were often tumultuous and seemed to change quickly from day to day. That is, a couple could have a serious fight one night, and yet everything could be calm and back together the next day. The reverse was also true.[6]

Divorce seemed to be simply a part of life. "That's just the way things are." Marriage is no bed of roses and "heartache is just part of life."[7]

Married women sometimes described themselves as trapped, trapped in a marriage with a husband who drops off to have a few beers before coming home from work, trapped with children and home responsibilities. One young woman put it this way,

> "Fred likes to drink. In fact, he drinks two or three six-packs sometimes before he comes home. By the time he gets home he's so drunk he don't know what he's doing. He's drunk right now. He had a six-pack or so before he came home, and now he is gone. That's why I say I'm trapped. . . . Like a bird in a cage. Here all day. Can't leave because of the two kids."[8]

She looked longingly at the motorcycle gangs. To her they were fun and "really a thrill." "I'd like to be riding right now on the back of one of them big bikes with the Bandits [a gang]. That's freedom—riding on the back of a big bike."[9] She soon left her husband and family to join the toughest gang in the area.

Not all women, of course, join motorcycle gangs or leave their families. But some of the women in Howell's study defend the necessity of "a fling." One woman expressed her feelings about it:

> "I tell you this—and so help me this is the truth—every woman, every woman wants to have her fling. Every woman that I know wants to have a fling and most women have a fling. It's just something about women, I don't know what it is. I don't know

how men feel; whether men have that or not. But it's the woman's fling that's the important thing."[10]

Obviously, the men have their own extramarital excursions. Wives and the children are suddenly left to fend for themselves when the husband takes off.

3. *Toughness.* The hard-living people of Clay Street saw themselves as fighters, as strong, independent people who would not let others push them around. It meant standing up to and telling off welfare workers, doctors, and other professional types. It meant telling the boss where to go. It sometimes meant fights. To be a fighter was to be tough.

A few of the people were really tough *and* violent. Neighbors reported that these people had actually beaten people to death. However, these were extreme cases, and most people tried mainly to convey an *image* of toughness. "For most people, toughness was only talk, and few actual fights or incidents occurred." Certain things were symbols of toughness, like "tough" cars, guns, and sexual exploits.[11]

The typical image was that of the tough guy, but women, too, could be strong and tough. Some were capable of hitting men with bricks or pans or clubs. One had once drawn a knife on a man who crossed her in a laundromat. One indicated that she had to be tough to survive. Another said, "If I wasn't a fighter I'd never of made it, not to say that I've really made it now. . . ."[12]

The people on Clay Street saw life as hard. To make it through life, a person had to be tough and able to fend for himself or herself. Yet one woman, in describing herself as a fighter, added, "Folks around here talk a big game, but really they ain't so tough. Not *underneath* they ain't."[13]

Howell concludes, "Underneath the tough image, I found most folks on Clay Street compassionate and sensitive." Underneath the rough exchange of words between couples, he found that humor, a twinkle of the eye, or a smile would transform "the harsh words to mean their opposite."[14]

4. *Political alienation.* For many of the hard-living people society is no good. It is under the control of the rich and the powerful who don't care about "the little man." Money is the

only thing that talks in this society, and the people with money, "they're the ones that tell the rest of us what to do."[15]

Most of the people on Clay Street do not vote and are not registered to vote. They think that politics is a waste of time and consists mainly of big deals to screw little people. The hard-living people feel they have too much on their minds to get involved, and, besides, "it don't really make a difference nohow."[16]

In spite of their severe problems, most did not make a connection between their own situation and the failure of government programs. Hard-living people were against government intrusion in their own lives. "They valued independence and self-reliance . . . and did not want government help . . . they wanted to succeed or fail on their own."[17]

The people of Clay Street had a basic ambivalence toward government. While they did not want its intrusion, they knew it existed, collecting taxes and spending their money. So they wondered why they did not get their fair share. This ambivalence led most people to believe that politics was irrelevant to their lives.

The alienation of hard-living people ran deeper than political issues. Expressions of alienation were found in hostility toward the church, professional people, government officials, the police, college students, and others who had "made it" or were "making it—the boss, white collar workers in general, rich folks."[18]

This alienation and hostility were related to the feeling that they were being exploited by the wider society. Not all of them used this feeling as an excuse for evading the law, and most of the people on Clay Street did not participate in widespread crime. What this alienation did do was condone the stealing that did take place, mostly from "big shots," not from each other. Thus it was not a matter of shame for those who got caught.[19]

Howell maintains that hard-living people are not really middle Americans or a part of the silent majority, seen as content with preserving the status quo. Hard-living people are different. They feel isolated, left out, scorned, and looked down on by more affluent whites. They are the forgotten Americans.

Stereotyped as "rednecks" by white liberals and many other professionals, they were confused and uncertain as to who they were. Accused by the press and others of being racists and bigots, they were bewildered by the labels and by the hostility they received. In their own view, they just wanted to keep their local school open. They were apprehensive of blacks moving into their neighborhoods or fearful that they would lose their jobs to blacks. They could not see why this was so wrong, why they were such barriers to "progress." Moreover, they wondered why *they* did not receive respectful treatment from the government and why *they* could not get adequate legal help and medical care at a cost they could afford.

Most hard-living people did not really want help from government. Mainly they wanted to be left alone. Yet, during hard times they felt the government cheated and ignored them.

5. *Rootlessness.* The hard-living families on Clay Street rarely were permanently settled. It was not unusual for a family to move six or eight times in ten years of marriage.

This impermanence of residence was interrelated with instability in other parts of their lives. If someone lost a job, this could intensify marital problems that could lead to separation or divorce. Marital stress, in turn, led to heavier drinking, days away from work, and a job loss. "A separation usually meant both partners went in search of new homes, giving up past friendships. A job loss meant failure to pay the rent, an eviction, more marital strain, etc."[20]

Most of the people of Clay Street were from the country or small towns. The city was not home, and they did not like to think of themselves as being there permanently. Many of them wanted to go back home, but not many ever did. And those few who went home found life more difficult there than in Washington. The hard-living people of Clay Street had kinfolk in Washington, in the rural South, and in towns in the region, but they were not close to these relatives. There was, to be sure, a nostalgia for home, but "there was no real 'home' to return to. . . ."[21]

As a result of this rootlessness, personal relationships took basically two forms. One of these was to "stick to themselves," to avoid much neighborhood contact. The other was to develop close relationships very quickly. Howell found this latter pattern to be the more basic one. He had been warned by a sociologist "that working-class people were very closed, family-oriented, and quite suspicious of strangers. On Clay Street nothing could have been further from the truth."[22] As quickly as these relationships formed, so they could end abruptly. When they were over, they were over. "That is the way life is." Warm and intense as the relationships were, they were not permanent.

Another result of the rootlessness was the absence of participation in community organizations. Few went to church or belonged to any formal clubs or groups. They had too much on their minds or too much to do to participate. They also expressed little interest in community affairs. However, the proposal to close the neighborhood school brought a furious attendance at the public hearing and with that the dropping of the plan. Howell concludes, "The hard living families were not against community involvement per se. It was just that they felt few community issues affected their lives and few community groups offered them much."[23] The school issue was an exception.

6. *Present time orientation.* "Life on Clay Street was intense, episodic, and preoccupied with the present." In order to plan for a future, people have to have one. But for hard-living people the future seemed "unpredictable, uncertain, and not very promising."[24] Some of the people, especially women, were trapped. They had no viable way, in their circumstances, of changing their situations. They had no energy to plan alternatives; it was tough enough just to make it through the day. Thus, the present time orientation grew from a generalized uncertainty about the future and from overwhelming personal problems.

It also had to do with getting something out of life when one could. Thus immediate gratifications were felt to be important.

At other times, however, the people of Clay Street expressed deep feelings of personal failure and talked of dreams they had for the future, a future of being settled down, a stable life. Yet while they said one thing, they did the exact opposite; that is, they engaged in the kinds of activities guaranteed to destroy their dreams. The gap between their words and deeds was no greater than that between their dreams and their ability to fulfill them. They wanted the symbols of being a typical, ordinary American: ranch house, car, color TV, dishwasher, furniture. But buying these symbols meant high monthly payments with no money left over for anything else. Such expense produced greater strain in the family and exacerbated other problems at home or on the job.[25]

7. *A strong sense of individualism.* Independence and self-reliance were highly valued by the hard-living people on Clay Street. "I like to do things *my* way." Their individualism was manifested in the clothes they wore, their cars and pickups, the way they talked, and especially in their attitudes toward work.

Most of the men had skills and saw themselves as craftsmen. They and their wives were proud of their abilities and skills. Others had no skills and expressed dissatisfaction with their jobs. In these cases pursuit of a skill was an important goal, a goal that those possessing skills usually had achieved on their own by using their wits.

A skill was important because skilled work was more rewarding, skilled jobs paid more, and the skilled workman had more independence. The men hated and shunned factory work because "you had to take orders all day and had no freedom."[26] They dreamed of jobs and positions in which they gave orders rather than taking them.

Because work was so important to the men, those without work or who were unable to work had a difficult adjustment: "I just don't feel right without my work. I don't know what to do with myself. It's not like me to drink like this. I usually don't drink when I've got work to do."[27]

Their individualism also expressed itself in a "basic way of viewing the world which distinguished between the general rule and the individual or special case." For example, the people on Clay Street were against people in general who were on welfare, but they tended to look at each individual case on its own merits. They were highly suspicious of white-collar executives and professionals and of government officials and political leaders in general, but certain individual employers or politicians were seen to be fine people.

Blacks were seen to be a definite threat to their jobs, their neighborhoods, and their position in society. Hard-living people's language was often scurrilously racist. Yet they spoke warmly and appreciatively of blacks who were co-workers, friends, and teachers. Tension existed between blacks and whites on Clay Street; yet there was tolerance for individual persons.

They were used to dealing with persons. What they were not used to was dealing with the wide range of bureaucracies, agencies, and corporations and their legal and organizational complications. When complications got in the way of receiving unemployment insurance, workmen's compensation, or Medicaid, they often responded by not battling the system. One man said, "If I can't get workmen's compensation, the hell with it. The government will screw you every time."[28]

In conclusion, hard living means heavy drinking, marital instability, toughness, political alienation, rootlessness, present time orientation, and a strong sense of individualism that prizes independence and self-reliance. Hard-living people are the people often called "rednecks" or "poor white trash." They are at the bottom of the working-class world.

Of all working-class people they tend to be the least involved in voluntary organizations of any kind. For this and other reasons they represent as difficult a challenge as the church faces when building relationships.

Part III

The Church and
the Blue-Collar American

8

The Religious Participation
of Blue-Collar People

Working-class people have turned to religion for help in their struggle with the crunch between achievement myths and blue-collar realities. At times religion has been powerfully compensative, that is, it has offered rewards in the spiritual realm in place of what has been denied in the live-a-day-at-a-time world. Sometimes religion has functioned as little more than an opiate, anesthetizing the pain of the work, the hardship, and the futility of life. Yet, the religious faith of working-class people cannot be reduced simply to economic or other factors alone because one also finds authentic belief and practice that inspire courage and commitment in the face of the challenges of working-class life. So what follows is an attempt to describe, in broad brush strokes, the religious expression of working-class people.

It would be simplest if I could take the four life-styles characterized in Part II and describe the religious expression of each one. Except for scattered references to religion in Part II, however, the studies did not focus on this facet of blue-collar life. What this chapter will do, then, is to look first at the people who do *not* go to church and their reasons. Then the discussion will turn to the religious expressions of blue-collar people. Finally, at the close of the chapter, I will venture a few generalizations about the church participation of winners, respectables, survivors, and hard livers.

Alienation and the Unchurched

J. Russell Hale suggests that poor church attendance may be the reflection of something deeply rooted in the culture rather than in the churches. "To be outside the churches in America may also be to be apart from other community-building enterprises, associations, and institutions in our society."[1] Hale cites the parallel findings of two studies that report that those not involved in the life of the church are also less likely to participate in any type of organization. In one of these two studies three-fourths of the unchurched did not claim membership in any voluntary organization.[2] Studies show that unchurched people tend to move more often than the churched and to have more shallow roots in their communities. The marginality of the unchurched may thus reflect a more pervasive cultural marginality.

Of the studies used in Part II, Howell's study on hard living provides the best illustration of this marginality of alienation. Howell found that most hard-living people are religious. They believe in God and some—with greater assurance—believe in hell, the place to which they see themselves headed with certainty. This envisagement is claimed as one reason for taking full advantage of life. Not only does a person live just once, but the punishment that awaits at the end of life seems to call for all the gusto *now* that one can muster.

Al, one of the men Howell got to know in his study, sent off for papers to become a preacher.

Al said, "Well, I've been living in sin too long and now I'm going to live right and be a minister of God."

Daisey said, "You're going to burn in hell, that's what you're going to do. . . ."

"I may burn in hell, but this ain't the worst thing I've done. Shit, I've broken every commandment there is. Says you can't commit adultery. Goddamn, no telling how many times I've committed adultery. Says you shouldn't rob. . . . I've robbed, I've stealed, I've coveted. I've coveted my neighbor's wife many a time. I mean there ain't much I haven't done. Why not add one more?"

Daisey said, "Well, as I said before, what you're doing now is the worst kind of sin, making fun of God."

Barney [another man present] said, "Well, you better make fun of Him now 'cause when you die, you and me is going to burn in hell."[3]

Although most hard-living people are religious, most of them are not church members. The attitude toward the church can be expressed in a number of comments frequently heard: "The church is crooked and a waste of time." "The church is full of a bunch of hypocrites." "Church people care more about what you wear to church than they do about you." "Church people don't give a damn about you." "Most ministers are phoney. They just sit back and take people's money. They don't do a goddamn thing." "Now I believe in God and all that, but I ain't got no use for the church."[4]

These are telling comments. Too often church people become defensive and accuse those who make such comments of making excuses for not participating in church. Perhaps this is true. Yet a good deal can be found in these comments if one resists being defensive and listens.

Basic to each of the six statements above is the indignity some people experience or at least feel in relationship to the church *and* to the larger community. This is most readily seen in the comments that are explicit about the church's incapacity to care about them. Survivors and hard livers feel demeaned by the church, just as they do by so much of the wider society. The indignities of class include the church's rejection of them.

Blue collarites complain that the church is more interested in the clothes people wear than in the condition of people's souls or the quality of their character. This is clearly a matter of not getting respect, of feeling that one is "looked down on." The clothing issue is not only one of money, how much the clothing costs; it is also one of taste. Standards of dress that are not their own are imposed on working-class people. They do not usually understand the standards for the simple reason that such standards are not operative in their own life-styles.

In the social encounters they have with people in higher class positions, they feel judged and found wanting on the basis of criteria that are external to them as individuals. Yet these standards seem to rule.

When this situation is experienced in church, it becomes clear that the church is not "theirs." It belongs to others. God may love them, but the church does not. For this reason and other similar experiences the church is charged with hypocrisy and crookedness. Marginal, alienated people know that the church is supposed to care, but the church conveys rejection by an indignity of class.

The attitude toward clergy—"They don't do a goddam thing"—translated means "They do not do anything for me." Persons are either ignored or put down. They are ignored because pastors usually spend more time with people whose life-style is similar to their own. Persons are put down by the subtleties of giving and getting respect in greetings and conversations. The put-downs come in the pastor's vocabulary, grammatical usage, gestures, and type of experiences recounted. What comes through is that the minister is not their kind of people. The minister "puts on airs." He or she is seen as "uppity" and, hence, phoney.

Another reason for believing that the clergy "don't do a damned thing" is that many blue-collar people work hard—*physically* hard—for a living. What they see clergy do looks like a piece of cake. They see the clean, well-appointed office of a pastor and note the fact that much of the pastor's work is done sitting down.

To be sure, the resentment toward this way of earning a living extends to many professional and managerial people, not to pastors only. But this qualification simply points out the pervasiveness of the alienation. Such alienation is not limited to one blue-collar life-style, although hard living is one of the clearest expressions of it.

Reaching out to alienated blue-collar people will be difficult for the church to do. How this can be done and where will be discussed in a later chapter. For now, attention turns to those who are active in church and how their religious beliefs and practices are lived out.

Blue-Collar Religious Expression

Among blue-collar people certain characteristics of religious expression have been recorded in social science literature over a good many years. In this section we shall look at blue-collar religiosity and delineate the characteristics most firmly established by these studies.

Believing and Feeling

When I worked my way through college as a roustabout in the oil fields of Mississippi, Snooks Britt knew that I was in college to become a preacher, and he delighted in setting traps for me. One day we were laying a pipeline through a swamp. As we were working, he asked me if I believed in the virgin birth.

By then I had had a course or two in Bible and philosophy of religion and possessed heady academic status as a partially educated fool. I replied, "Well, Snooks, first, you've got to compare those passages in the New Testament with those in the Old; then, you've got to look at the cultural context and what it meant to be a divine-human. . . ." That's as far as I got.

"Wahharrr," his favorite expression, "college boy, I didn't ask you what you *thought;* I asked you what you *believed!*" It took me fifteen years to appreciate the significance of what he was talking about.

The Lynds in their 1929 study of Muncie, Indiana, found that "members of the working class show a disposition to believe their religion more ardently and to accumulate more emotionally charged values around their beliefs."[5]

In contrast middle-class people are more likely to *think* and *know* their religion. They tend to be more interested in religious knowledge and in studying and thinking about their religious views.

Sociological studies reveal that blue-collar people tend to: have a strong feeling or experiential dimension in their religious expression; have a strong devotion to doctrine, a creedalism—such as Snooks's interest in the virgin birth—that exhibits greater commitment to religious belief; have greater interest in matters that are especially religious and non-secular in content.[6]

This strong creedal orientation of blue collarites poses some problems. They hold their beliefs so strongly that they are found to be more intolerant about religion than people from the middle and upper classes. For example, blue-collar people are less tolerant of an atheist's right to speak at a public meeting, to have his or her book in the public library, or to teach in a college. It needs to be said, however, that while intolerance is more pronounced among working-class people, those who gave intolerant answers were still a minority of the blue-collar people who responded to questions. The majority of blue-collar people were more tolerant.[7]

Communal Attachment

The second characteristic of blue-collar religious expression is a strong communal orientation and relationship. This means that blue-collar people tend to have "close personal bonds within the church"[8] Many of their close friends and relatives are members.[9] I remember a couples club in a church I once served that was, in fact, a friendship and kinship group that had been together for about ten years. Some of the members had been members at that church thirty years or more. One of the women in the group said, "We're just old chums, and this is our church."

For blue collarites like these the church is not an association, not a secondary social relationship; it is a community. Their involvement is communal. The church serves as a primary group for them. Charles H. Cooley's definition of a primary group is a group in which people know one another well and in which there is a sense of "wholeness." Members of such a group form a "we." They have a common identity and profound sympathy for one another. They share each other's joys and woes.[10]

This church communal relationship can be further understood by contrasting it with the relationship in a church whose membership is primarily an audience. That church is made up of people who get together primarily to worship and so are not bonded by close personal ties.[11] As I shall show in the next chapter the communal character of blue-collar religious expression has important implications for the ministry of the church.

Church Attendance

The third characteristic of religious expression concerns the attendance of working-class people at religious services. The stereotype of blue-collar people is that they do not go to church. While they may be religious, they do not participate actively in church services and other organizational activities. Middle- and upper-class people are more likely to express their religion this way, at least so the stereotype goes.

This stereotype does not hold up. One study divided the United States populace into four strata: upper class, middle class, working class, and lower class. People in these four strata were then asked whether they attended church "regularly," "often," "some," or "rarely." The findings of this study indicate that working-class people and lower-class people attend church with the same frequency as the rest of the population. A full third of working-class people report that they attend church regularly. This is only slightly less than the number of middle-class church attenders and roughly the same as the upper class. The percentage of lower-class people attending "regularly" is greater than the percentage of upper-class people and about the same as the middle class.[12]

Working-class people vary from the other class groups in their high percentage of people who attend "rarely." While a third of the working class attends church regularly, 29 percent report that they go "rarely." Thus working-class people are more likely to go to church often or to go hardly at all.[13]

Blue-collar church attendance also varies by denomination. Sect groups and the Roman Catholic Church have the highest percentage of blue collarites who attend regularly. Methodists, Lutherans, and Baptists reflect the pattern of blue-collar attendance for the nation as a whole with 20 to 30 percent of blue-collarites attending regularly. Blue-collar Presbyterians and Episcopalians have the highest percentages attending "rarely."

Among lower-class people, again, the sects and the Roman Catholics have the highest percentage of those attending "regularly." The lowest attendance rate is found in the Lutheran, Presbyterian, and Episcopal denominations.[14]

Finally, it is quite clear that a larger number of blue-collar women than blue-collar men attend church. The difference, however, is not a result of class since this pattern of church attendance by men and women is found throughout the class structure. The small differences in statistics between class levels that do exist are not significant.[15]

Religious Affiliation

There are no clear-cut working-class or lower-class denominations. The high status denominations have a significant proportion of blue-collar people in their membership, and even the sects have upper-class members, a fact that probably indicates the upward mobility of a number of the sect groups.

The denominations with the highest percentage of working-class members are the Lutherans, the Baptists, and the Methodists, followed by the sects, the Roman Catholics, the Episcopalians, and the Presbyterians. In regard to lower-class members, the Baptists and the sects have the highest percentages, and Episcopalians and Lutherans have the lowest. Moreover, it appears that this relationship between social class and religious affiliation has remained essentially the same for twenty-five years.[16]

Strength of Religious Preference

Blue-collar people seem to identify more intently with their denominations and to hold on to their preferences more strongly than other classes. It should be said, however, that no class has a majority of its people claiming intense affiliation.

Among the four strata delineated previously, the lower class seems to hold religious preferences most intently (46.9 percent), followed by the working class (40.6 percent), the upper class (37.9 percent) and the middle class. Only a little over a fourth of the middle-class respondents reported strong religious preference.

Intensity of religious preference also seems to vary by denomination. Lower-class Episcopalians, Presbyterians, and especially, sectarians report strong religious preferences. In the working class the Catholics and Lutherans report stronger preference.[17]

In sum, the studies on affiliation and denominational preference suggest that while blue-collar people are found in all denominations, some denominations have a great representation of blue-collar people. And working-class people and especially lower-class people hold stronger preference for the church group to which they belong. This varies from one denomination to another.

Type of Congregation

Finally, blue-collar people seem to be more active in certain *types* of churches. A study of Gastonia categorized local religious groups into five types: uptown, transitional, middle class, sect, and black.[18] The distribution of blue-collar people varied significantly by type of church. These five types are described below.

1. *The uptown church,* located in the center of the city, typically drew its membership of more than 1,000 from all over the city. It possessed a large sanctuary and complete educational facilities and was staffed by two or three full-time pastors and other staff. The church itself was dominated by upper-class and upper middle-class families. A large proportion of the congregation was college-educated.[19]

2. *The transitional church* got its start in a mill village in the twenties and thirties. The majority of the churches were Baptist or Methodist, and their memberships were usually about five hundred people. The mostly upper blue-collar members had varied income and educational levels and their homes no longer clustered around the church building. They often lived several miles away and bypassed churches of the same denomination to attend worship at the transitional church. The church buildings were new and well-kept, small-scale ver-

sions of large uptown church buildings. Usually these churches had one or two pastors, a secretary, and many volunteers. The congregation itself was composed primarily of mill workers or former mill workers who now lived in middle-class suburban areas. Neither a mill nor an uptown congregation, the transition church integrated aspects of each.[20]

3. *The middle-class church* was a suburban church and developed with the industrialization following World War II. It typically had about 350 members and a newly constructed building that was hardly ever adequate. A pastor and a part-time seminary student typically made up the staff. Without long-standing traditions or forms of practice, these churches emphasized fellowship and participation in relatively informal programs.

Reflecting the occupational diversity of its neighborhood, the middle-class church was dominated by neither white-collar nor blue-collar families. The membership lived around the church, and only a minority commuted from other areas. In terms of social class these churches were "the most diverse, inclusive, and heterogeneous of the churches—perhaps of all organized groups—in the community."[21] The mixture of white-collar people and blue-collar people prevented it from being the supporter of the status quo that the uptown church was, but it was not likely that one of these churches would pose a serious threat to the dominant order.

4. *The sect church* had been an important part of Gastonia's religious life since its earliest days; "mill churches, regardless of denomination, were frequently sectarian in character."[22] These sectarian groups were dominated by mill workers or unskilled workers in mill-related industries. The socially marginal and the poor had especially sought out sect groups. The sect participants were local residents who attended services in inexpensive facilities near their homes. The sect buildings were usually of concrete-block construction, or they were the old church buildings abandoned or sold by other religious groups. The churches usually had an auditorium but no educational facilities. The preacher often had only a grammar school ed-

ucation and may have taken correspondence courses from a Bible institute of some kind.

The services of worship were "frequent, long and led by any one of several people."[23] The service of worship was designed not so much to communicate a message as to convoke a religious experience. Participants were called to "be free" in the service, to experience the euphoria of "feeling at liberty" without being confined by structure or formality. Yet the activities seemed somewhat contrived, a kind of "patterned spontaneity." The sect was a religious outlet providing its members a "sense of community, participation and euphoria not present in the more formal service." With their poor organization and meager resources, the sects represented no challenge to the established order, and "their understanding of social reality [was] privatistic, nearly synonymous to that of their uptown counterparts."[24]

5. *The black church* in Gastonia has greater prominence now than in 1939 (when Pope studied it) "due largely to the role these groups played during the civil rights struggles of the 1960s. Black churches virtually span the sociological categories used for white churches."[25] The larger, stable black churches had memberships of several hundred and were highly organized. In the black "uptown" churches the clergy all had college and seminary degrees. The pastor and a volunteer secretary with volunteer workers constituted the staff of the uptown black church. The lay leaders in these churches were professionals and white-collar workers, but more than two-thirds of their membership were constituted of lower blue-collar workers. This kind of social diversity was not found among any of Gastonia's white churches or among the black sect groups. In contrast, the black sect churches were small and struggling, and their viability depended upon the energy and charisma of their leaders. Their pastors were typically poorly educated.[26]

In this study of Gastonia the sect church had the largest percentage of blue-collar people, followed by the transitional church, the middle-class church, and the black church. Uptown churches had the smallest percentage of blue-collar workers.

Membership in these Gastonia churches also varied by *type* of blue-collar worker. Sects were dominated by operatives and similar workers. In the black churches, laborers were the largest occupational category. The largest proportion of craftworkers, forepersons, and such was found in the transitional churches where they were also the largest single occupational category. Craftworkers and forepersons were also the largest group of blue-collar workers in middle-class churches where they were second only to managers, officials, and proprietors as the major occupational group in the membership. In the uptown churches craftworkers and forepersons constituted well over half of the blue-collar workers who were members.

Obviously this distribution of blue-collar workers by type of congregation comes from one study only. In all likelihood it is not adequately representative of the United States, especially since Gastonia is located in the southeastern part of the country where people tend to participate more actively in churches. However, this typology of congregations is still a useful tool for examining the church participation of blue-collar people because the general distribution of the types of congregation seems to match up with certain residential patterns of the working class.

The suburbanization of the United States has had a significant impact on the residential patterns of working-class people and, therefore, on the type of churches to which they belong. Even though the occupational distributions and proportions in these churches may vary from the findings in Gastonia, related developments in residential patterns and church membership and participation can be found across the country. For mainline denominations this means that their best means of reaching blue-collar people will be in transitional and middle-class churches. Furthermore, members of these churches will typically be blue-collar winners and respectables.

One other type of church, not classified in the previous typology, often has a high proportion of blue-collar members. This is the *neighborhood church* whose members live within walking distance of the building. Closely identified with the neighborhood, the church is frequently found in an older residential area. The church participants who live outside the neighborhood once lived in the neighborhood or attend the church because of family ties or both. The neighborhood church has two hundred members or so and is served by a young minister fresh out of seminary, a student minister, or a retired one. This church is a communal group, not an association or audience, and the members' ties to it are deep and abiding. These churches endure because their people see their church as an extension of themselves and their relationships.

Recent studies on the small church are quite helpful in understanding these neighborhood congregations. Carl Dudley describes the small church as a "single, caring cell embracing the whole congregation." In these churches everyone knows one another on an ongoing face-to-face basis. "The caring cell church may be defined as a primary group in which the members expect to know, or know about, all other members."[27] Dudley points out that in such primary groups people are held together by "common interests, beliefs, tasks, and territory." Their relationships are not contractual but sentimental. Their solidarity is based on a sense of belonging, which is sustained by "experiences of intimacy and personal need."[28] These churches can be seen as extended families.

Lyle Schaller has recently argued that "the small-membership congregation is a different *type* of religious institution than the larger churches."[29] Among these differences are: its ministry of the laity and its dependence on volunteers, its orientation toward people rather than performance, its need for and positive use of the grapevine, its intergenerational groupings, its relational and interpersonal rather than functional approaches to church life, its participatory democratic style, and its use of an "internal" clock and its own special calendar. The literature on the small church is an important resource for working with blue-collar people in neighborhood congregations.[30]

In sum, blue-collar church people are strongly oriented toward believing and feeling their faith and tend to be communally involved in their religious groups. They do attend church and constitute significant proportions of the membership of all

denominations in the United States, especially the sects. Moreover, they hold stronger and more intense denominational preferences than do middle-class and upper-class people generally.
Their participation varies by denomination and by type of
church, with their presence proportionally larger in middle-
class, transitional, sect, and neighborhood churches.

Blue-Collar Life-Styles and Religious Expression

Now I want to venture some tentative generalizations about
blue-collar life-styles and blue-collar church participation. It
seems fairly clear that the respectables are the people most
likely to participate in the churches. They are the conformists,
the ones who have bought into the system. They seem the least
alienated although they may also be the ones who work hardest
to avoid marginality. The strain of that effort is reflected, in
part, in authoritarian attitudes and behavior, but such attitudes and behaviors characterize a minority of the respectables.
Respectables are the shock troops of blue-collar church members. They will be found in any congregation with working-
class people.

Blue-collar winners are typically in jobs as craftworkers,
forepersons, and such. The study of Gastonia found these occupations significantly represented in transitional churches,
followed by middle-class churches and then sects. While they
constitute the largest group of blue-collar people in uptown
churches, they form a smaller proportion of these church memberships in any except black churches.

Operatives and similar workers participated overwhelmingly in sect churches (almost 45 percent) in Gastonia. I suspect
that this pattern would be found among blue-collar survivors
around the country, although the proportion may shift from
place to place. One should also expect to find many respectables
in the sects.

Hard-living people are least likely to participate in the church.
They are the most alienated and marginal. Yet even here

Howell reports that some of the hard-living people he knew moved into churches, especially the sects.

The church will have its best chance of attracting working-class people to membership and participation if it is able to respond genuinely to their needs and to do so in a manner consistent with their forms of religious expression.

9

The Church and
the Blue-Collar American

It is clear that blue-collar people actively participate in the churches and constitute significant proportions of virtually all denominations. In light of this we need to return to the religion of winning and ask what relationship the religion of churches has to this dominant civil religion. Or, to put it another way, what function does religious expression perform in coping with the gap between achievement myths and blue-collar realities?

Glock, Ringer, and Babbie in their study of Episcopalians contend that the church represents an "alternative source of gratification."[1] In the case of lower-status women, the church provides the status gratification that is denied in secular society. Men, whatever the class, participate in church less than women, and "while the effect of social class is not as strong, a similar conclusion may be reached."[2] Hence, "involvement in a prestigious church such as the Protestant Episcopal may serve to alleviate the unfulfilled status needs of lower class members," and the church may offer a refuge for those who are denied material wealth and high social status.[3]

In his study of Lutherans, Demerath characterizes the religious expressions of lower-status people as sectlike, that is, they have a devotion to doctrine, a propensity to spontaneous religious expression, and a sense of being a distinct moral community. He sees this sectlike expression, in contrast to churchlike expressions, arising out of the secular needs of lower-status people.

> Because of its emphatic rejection of those secular values which separate the "achievers" from the "nonachievers"—the "success-ful" from the "unsuccessful"—the sect has historically been a haven for the socially depressed and the socially isolated. The sect provides a community in which all are equally the children of God. Thus, the secular circumstances of the lower classes tend to propel them into sects. These same secular circumstances also serve to make the lower social strata in our society more sectlike in their orientation regardless of their formal religious affilia-tion.[4]

Stark, in a more recent review of the issues of religious commitment and social class, sees economically deprived church participants involved in activities that meet their deprivation needs. The church participation of middle-class and upper-class people validates their secular success. Involvement in the church demonstrates that one is "respectable, substantial, responsible, and proper."[5] However, the comfort and support that lower-status people need come from a strong traditional faith, an active prayer life, and deep emotional experiences.

There can be little doubt that the form blue-collar religious expression takes is influenced by deprivation. And at least in part, the religion of the churches is one way of dealing with the winner religion of the culture.

Not only is religion compensative for working-class people, some evidence suggests that it is highly segmented from the rest of life. In their study Sennett and Cobb "found organized religion little on the minds of workingmen, and all attempts to raise the issue in relation to work, feelings of personal adequacy, and the like, fell flat." For the men and women they interviewed, religion was a "distinct compartment of their lives, ... an obligatory role separate from the obligations of class."[6]

Demerath, in his *Social Class in American Protestantism,* developed this segmentation theme even further. His findings are summarized in three points. First, the lower that one's secular status is, the more apt one is to seek out institutions with unique values as a framework for interaction and self-judgment. Second, within any institution those lower in status are more likely to seek out the least secular facets as the focus of their commitment. And, third, it is possible to gain a suitably distinct orientation in organizations other than church.[7]

These findings by Demerath are not hopeful in terms of blue-collar church people exerting influence on the secular issues before them. This is corroborated by Glock and Stark who contend that the more one seeks radical change, the less likely one is to be involved in a church or sect; that the more deeply one is involved in the church, the less likely one is to seek radical change. "Religious and radical commitments are mutually corrosive."[8]

What does all of this mean? Simply this: religion is important to blue-collar people as a compensative and alternative way of meeting needs unanswered in secular society. However, religion seems to be segmented from the issues of winner culture and inequality and their impact on blue-collar life ways. The result is that the church, with its unique values and nonsecular orientations for working people, becomes an unlikely arena for addressing the systemic issues confronting blue-collar America unless the church departs from typical modes of operating.

Thus, these questions arise: Can the church—especially the local church—have any effect on these systemic issues? Is there a response that takes into account the characteristic religious expressions of working-class people and the special problems of religious segmentation in ways that have secular impact? These questions are the focus of this chapter.

Theological Response

The first response of the church could be a response consistent with blue-collar religious expression and aimed directly at winner religion. That is, a direct assault on winner religion not only could offer a challenge to the achievement culture but also provide the kind of unique, nonsecular religious beliefs and values that appeal to working-class church people.

The Christian faith provides a theological response that could challenge winner religion and offer a clear, nonsecular alternative to it. The Christian faith deals with the issue of human dignity and proposes a vision of what it means to be human. Both of these are live issues today. They can be addressed by a theology of grace and a vision of human destiny as the completion or fulfillment of God's purposes.

Theology of Grace

Winner religion places people in a contest for dignity, a striving for worth and value. In Part I, I made the case that this is an incessant and, finally, futile striving because worth cannot be earned.

A theology of grace takes an opposite position in respect to human worth. Human worth is not earned; it comes as a gracious gift from God in Jesus Christ. In this sense a gospel of grace challenges the very foundation of achievement values. Worth is not a prize won through endless strife but is a gift from God that one receives by trusting and accepting it. In Paul's terms this is justification by faith through grace, that is, one is made right and worthy through God's love, which is received by faith, a trusting acceptance of the gift.

A grace theology undercuts the division of the world into winners and losers and proclaims that all people are subjects of God's love and, therefore, of infinite worth, altogether apart from who they are and what they have done. For this reason an authentic gospel of grace is a powerful leveler. It calls into question rituals of deference built on inequalities of respect and dignity. It challenges distributions of power in which the few control the many. And it speaks to the experience of failure perhaps more powerfully than can anything else—especially winning—because it shatters the equation of failure equals worthlessness.

When people are set free from the contest for dignity, they are no longer tied to a fruitless quest, and their energies are not dissipated in the inherent psychic conflicts of winner religion. For this reason a gospel of grace fuels a more authentic quest to be and to become fully human. We turn now to that.

A New Vision of Humanness

In winner religion the vision of what it means to be human is to be a winner, to be number one. As I have shown, it is an inhuman vision. Its competitive individualism sets neighbor against neighbor, justifies social inequalities and—to make matters even worse—is not fair competition.

Christian faith offers an alternative, which can be expressed in an old-fashioned but important word: sanctification. It does not mean "sanctimonious" as one might initially think. Rather, the word has two meanings, which I shall examine here. The first meaning of "sanctification" is "to be made whole, to be completed, or, at least, to be in the process of being completed." The word applies not only to individuals but to society as well. Actually, it applies to the whole of creation, which God takes to completion and fulfillment. So sanctification is not an individualistic process, but a process in which the infinite worth of each person is placed in a larger corporate and cosmic whole.

Such a vision has the potential to reverse the field of an achievement culture. The aim of life is no longer for each person to be number one, but for each person to contribute to the completion of self, community, and creation. The goal is no longer to get to the top but, rather, to discover and fulfill the special qualities of each person and each community in the context of a creation whose destiny is consummation in God. The vision's images are not competition but completion, not winning but wholeness.

One concrete illustration suggests the difference this understanding could make. It is no secret that older people are not highly valued in an achievement culture. One of the basic reasons for this is because when one is old, one can be only one of two things: either a "has-been" or a "never-was." In a culture in which completing life fulfills its vision of what it means to be human, aging increases the richness of each individual's life, and older people will be appreciated as those who bear such treasure.

The second meaning of "sanctification" is "to be set apart for God's work, to have a special mission in the world," not a mission of privilege but—clearly stated in the New Testament—of servanthood. To be sanctified in this sense is to become the people of God—not in the exclusive sense meaning to be the only people God cares about, but in the sense of being people with a special responsibility to reach out to the world God loves.

When this second meaning of sanctification is combined with the first, the community of faith joins God in the completion of the creation. The community then has alternative beliefs and values to the winner attitude and a distinctive task.

Working-class people caught between achievement myths and blocked opportunities seek out institutions with unique values and gratification, especially those that are nonsecular. I am proposing that working-class people can find in the church an alternative source of status and that a gospel of grace offers just such an alternative orientation. It provides a unique set of nonsecular values in the context of a winner culture. It, therefore, fits in with the styles of blue-collar religious expression, but it goes beyond them because it offers a powerful interpretive and liberating word to people caught in an achievement culture. What we have here, then, is a faith perspective from which to construct a response by the church to blue-collar life, a faith perspective that is stylistically relevant and theologically sound. It challenges the established culture and speaks to the condition of working-class people.

A Church Style Befitting Blue-Collar People

However, theology is not enough. A theology of grace and a vision of human destiny as completion will remain abstractions unless they are embodied in communities of faith and empower working-class people.

I have reported that blue-collar people tend to segment religion from the rest of their lives. If the theological perspective I have offered remains compartmentalized in the church, it will be no more helpful than other approaches. Can this dividing wall of segmentation be brought down? If so, how? I will look for strategic directions in the church and in the community in order to answer these questions.

Believing and Feeling in Worship

Blue-collar people believe and feel their religion. This style of religious expression, therefore, will be important to a congregation that intends to relate meaningfully to blue-collar people. Preaching, for example, can be thoughtful, but it will require fervor and conviction in order to capture the appreciation of working-class people. When sermons are described by working-class people as "a talk" or, worse, as "a lecture," the preacher needs to understand that these are not compliments. Whatever he or she did, it was not preaching!

Believing and feeling must be reflected in the liturgy and would improve the worship life of many congregations! Some of what passes as theologically sophisticated liturgy is pretense and a mechanical imposition of prayers, litanies, and hymns that are "traditional" and singularly dull and opaque in language. Liturgy does not have to be upper middle class to be creative and renewing.

I remember well the liturgical violence that I, as the pastor, and an organist with a graduate degree in music once did to a working-class congregation. We were determined that these people would learn to appreciate Mozart, Bach, and Beethoven. A typical example was the way the organist played—with my unqualified support—and we sang the hymn "Joyful, Joyful, We Adore Thee," the tune of which comes from Beethoven's Ninth Symphony. The organist played it without pausing after each phrase or even after each verse—in the style of "sophisticated musicians." I remember that I often gasped at times, trying to find a place to breathe! And that congregation, which deserved better, on occasion simply looked exhausted.

The problem, of course, is that blue-collar people do not deserve that insensitivity. The new breed of clergy who bring in secular songs and singers, popular with the affluent, college-educated crowd, in order to be creative usually do not consider Loretta Lynn songs or Johnny Cash songs worthy of such "experimental excellence." The fact that Lynn and Cash speak with considerably more power to the conditions of working-class people does not enter the clergys' minds.

I suspect that there are plenty of theologically legitimate and ecclesiastically appropriate leads for liturgical depth in country and western music, for example, which so far the churches have barely touched. In a time when Americans have become interested in soul music, it is baffling that the soul music of white lower-class and working-class Americans should be neglected by the churches.

An important task in liturgy is the communication of the Good News of God's grace and the affirmation of the community of people gathered together. If the worship service is alien to the congregation, if it is an implicit—even if it is an unintended—putdown of their lives and circumstances, it is difficult to see how the proclaimed gracious love of God can be heard. The indignities of class have no place in the worship of God. Disparagement and rejection of working-class people in the church—even if by default—do not aid the people to come to terms with the discounting they inevitably experience in a class society.

Basically what is needed is a form of worship that reflects certain dimensions of a sect style and has an affirming and prophetic message. Believing and feeling can be an integral part of worship without a focus on "pie-in-the-sky," which often characterizes blue-collar worship. If the style of worship is authentic to blue-collar people, then the emphasis on pie-in-the-sky can be changed to a concern for a balanced diet in the here and now. This will not be an easy adjustment to make because religion for lower social classes typically provides an escape from the unfriendliness of the world rather than motivation and mobilizing force to lay claim to what is rightfully theirs.

An approach that has a strong biblical orientation will speak to the belief and orthodoxy interests of working-class people. And, if the biblical orientation is comprehensive and authentic, it will address the life experience of working-class people. Such an orientation will not serve as an opiate but will affirm the worth of persons and call them to respond and to make changes necessary for a more human life.

Church Programming in a Communal Setting

An effective church program will reflect the communal characteristic of blue-collar religious expression. Yet this seems to be another area in which middle-class—especially upwardly mobile—church clergy and professionals experience so much frustration. For example, the old Sunday church school class that has been meeting for twenty-five years and that has received so much criticism by frustrated pastors may be answering important needs because it does pull together a communal group and affirm the members.

Middle-class people tend to be associative in their relationship to the church, and this style is more amenable to middle-class church professionals. The middle-class professional with wide geographical mobility and a nexus of friends extending across a metropolitan area, or the nation even, does not usually find his or her primary relationships in a single group in the church. Rather, these church relationships are one set of a myriad of other relationships, and they tend to serve one set of needs.

For blue-collar people the communal group is a gathering of friends, a group of people one knows well and has known for a number of years. The pastor or other church professional sometimes misses the significance of these communal groups and may offend persons in the working class by his or her insensitivity.

The communal style has implications for church programming and administration that are quite different from those of the associational style. The differences relate closely to class.

Middle-class people are typically in jobs and relationships where committee meetings, planning, and verbal articulation of ideas are important. In contrast most working-class people do *physical* work for a living. Their decisions are often made for them or made in the context of a gang or work crew. Verbalization is not very important; in fact, many working-class people are suspicious of "talkers" because, in their experience, to talk is to malinger. Also, however one characterizes their work, committee work it is not, and they do not do much of the kind of planning that committee work entails.

Now, when a middle-class pastor devises programs in an associative style, the programs will be alien to many blue-collar people. They will see the approach of the people who give them orders, their bosses. To be sure, planning is necessary, but it needs to be done in a sensitive fashion. Otherwise it is an implicit—even explicit—put-down of working-class people.

Also, placing working-class people in an associational type of setting puts them at a disadvantage. When the premium is on talk, on vocabulary, on committee procedures, and *Robert's Rules of Order,* the situation is a setting to which they are not accustomed, and they are not likely to participate well. Some blue-collar people avoid such settings altogether. People in general do not like to be where they are at a disadvantage, and blue-collar people are no different.

What is needed, then, is an approach that is communal in its orientation. A communal approach has at least three characteristics. *First, a communal group operates more like a family than like an organization.* It is not primarily concerned with efficiency. It is not basically utilitarian in style. It is more interested in keeping the close bonds of relationship and deepening the ties of love. Most families meet and make decisions, but not in committee form. Communal groups act like families. They make extensive use of informal relationships and the opportunity for people to think about and talk about what needs to be done. Communal groups take into account the points of view of people who may not verbalize their positions in a meeting. Communal groups may take considerable time to make a decision because they want everyone to feel okay about it. Communal groups may place loyalty above what seems to be "the right thing to do." Communal groups are more intuitive. They have intrinsic value and are not prone to being used primarily as a means to another end.

Second, communal groups are not primarily goal oriented but rather are gathering oriented. Communal groups come together in order to *be* together. In this sense they are more oriented to belonging and being than to doing, although they will *do* a lot just to be together. These gatherings are a basic source of power in communal groups.

Perhaps the analysis of Emile Durkheim, the French sociologist, is most instructive here. For Durkheim, society itself was fundamentally a religious reality held together by a collective conscience. This conscience created a sense of belonging to a group or society and one felt duty bound to live up to that group's claims. Durkheim believed that society rested on a common religious moral order and not on a rational pursuit of self-interest.

While I do not fully accept Durkheim's view, his insight into how human solidarity is formed or how commitment to the collective conscience is generated and sustained is important for my purposes here. Durkheim contended that when people are *physically close together, focus their attention on a common object or event, and engage in exercises that arouse emotion, then bonding occurs.* Human solidarity is formed. From a sociological perspective, this is the function of religion.[9]

The gatherings of communal groups form and sustain solidarity. They are rituals that bond people together, and they cannot be reduced to rationalized, associational activities without losing their power to form and sustain community. Middle-class church professionals would do well to learn the significance of such rituals and, rather than battle them, work with them.

This means that a lot more is going on at a church supper than just eating. It means that a whole lot more is happening in the Young Couple's Sunday church school class—whose members are all over fifty—than just reading the lesson. These gatherings are the rituals of solidarity.

Third, the communal approach focuses not so much on program as on events. I am not satisfied with this distinction, what I am looking for is the difference between a banquet and a church supper, between a study group and a celebration, between a planned occasion and a happening. Events, as understood here, are less linear or calculated and more intuitive, spontaneous, and narrative in approach.

People like me, who have a special interest in liberation and social justice, are people who tend to be oriented toward ideas, concepts, workshops, strategy, and tactics. Perhaps one of the reasons that we have no more influence than we do—especially with blue-collar people—is that we have not sufficiently learned the power of gatherings and events. Any demonstration or march under the leadership of Martin Luther King, Jr., was preceded or succeeded by a stirring event that looked like a revival. Such an event bonded people together and empowered them to face the ordeal that lay ahead.

What are the implications of this communal approach to church life? Do these familylike rituals of solidarity suggest any directions for working in the blue-collar church? Some of the implications are quite clear. The gathering is the basic way to congregate working people. It is as basic a way to sustain community and to motivate and mobilize people as there is.

The power of a gathering, in the form of an event, is the best way to approach issues confronting working-class people. For example, the Rev. Lea Joyner is pastor of a church in Monroe, Louisiana, with over two thousand members, most of whom are blue-collar people. At one time in the area around the church friction existed between the police and the community. Many people in a situation like this attempt to set up a workshop on police and community relationships. Not Ms. Joyner. Instead she organized a celebration, a tea (!) honoring the police, and invited the entire community to come. It was such a success that it became an annual event.

She said, "I guess that sounds kind of simple, doesn't it? But, you know, if a policeman sees a teenager on the street and is tempted to exceed his authority, he wonders if the child was at the tea. And if a teenager is tempted to throw a rock at the police car, he wonders what if the policeman was at the tea?" The gathering created community.

A creative approach to the communal style of blue-collar church life will find many ways to present issues to the people and to respond to yearnings for community. The Rev. Richard Seaton, pastor of a blue-collar church in Kansas City with about three hundred members, led his church through an "End of the Summer Festival," a celebration organized very much like an old country fair. The fair had exhibits of canned goods and home produce, pet shows, hot dog and cotton candy stands, sponge-throwing contests, square dancing, and a host of other activities. The event was held on the church parking lot and the street next to it, which was roped off. There was a bandstand where local country music and country gospel bands played. The event lasted from 10 A.M. to 9 P.M. and drew a thousand people.

Seaton reports that this celebration was a very important part of the community's movement on certain social issues. This gathering brought people together, helped them get to know one another, and to express common concerns. As a result of this street festival, in part, the church participated very actively with the community in forming a housing association, a senior citizens center, and a voter registration program. The work of this church and its pastor indicates clearly the power and the relevance of gatherings and events to blue-collar people.

The communal style of blue-collar religious expression is a major resource for dealing with working-class realities. Paradoxically, it is this communal orientation that also is a key to breaking down the segmentation of the church and religious expression from community issues.

A Congregation of Congregations

As I showed in the previous chapter, blue-collar people can be found mainly in middle-class, transitional, neighborhood, and sect churches. In the transitional and middle-class churches, particularly, they are one part—a substantial part—of the congregation, with middle-class people being the dominant group. This means, obviously, that such churches cannot operate as though they were blue-collar or middle-class churches only. Thus the church will have to be pluralistic.

What appeals to middle-class people may not appeal to blue-collar people. Certainly programs and activities alien to blue-collar religious expression will appeal only to a few. As a result of this, churches will find it necessary to establish distinctive events and opportunities in order to attract and fulfill working-class people. Because of the middle-class bias of most pastors in these congregations, special care and attention to a communal style will be required because the tendencies will be to go in the other direction.

Each middle-class and transitional church is a congregation of congregations, and each congregation within the larger congregation has its own distinctive needs and style. This complexity poses a significant challenge to the pastor. How can he or she work in the midst of this diversity and discover a church role that relates meaningfully to blue-collar people, a role that is effective in the church and in the community? This is the concern of the next chapter in which I examine the role of the pastor as ward heeler.

10

The Pastor as Ward Heeler

Blue-collar people are present in churches in sizable proportions. Although they do not dominate most congregations
as do middle-class people, they do nevertheless constitute a
significant part of the plurality of many congregations. Moreover, blue-collar people are a diverse group themselves. This
diversity is expressed not only in the life-styles of blue-collar
winners, respectables, survivors, and hard livers, but also in
the life-styles of those who are involved in the church and those
who are not.

Such complexity poses a challenge to the pastor who wants
to relate effectively to the church and the community. Many
of the images of the pastor in current literature do not, in my
opinion, adequately fit this challenge. For example, the image
of an enabler has a middle-class resonance, and working-class
people both wince and chuckle over its use by unsuspecting
pastors. "Player-coach" has a ring of unreality about it. Its use
in the church and its connection with the situation blue-collar
people have at work give the label that amateur quality associated with people who are trying to be "with it" and who
obviously are not. And "processor"—for heaven's sake—will

make most working-class people think of a line job in a meat-packing plant!

Looking over the history of working-class people, one sees plenty of times when a great deal of complexity characterized their lives. In the late nineteenth and early twentieth centuries working-class sections of the cities teemed with ethnic and racial groups. The great waves of immigration from Europe filled the cities of the eastern United States with a patchwork quilt of ethnic neighborhoods. In these settings working-class people—most of them Catholic—found the prejudice and discrimination that every powerless group experiences in the United States. From these circumstances grew the political machines that challenged middle-class and—primarily—Protestant power. These political machines were the most effective groups in the history of the United States in working with blue-collar people, matched at times, perhaps, only by the labor unions and the Roman Catholic Church.

To be sure, these political organizations were also characterized by corruption, coercion, and violence. Yet a fair reading of American history would find that they were no more corrupt, coercive, and violent than the business and industrial power of the time. This is said not to justify the excesses of the political machines but, rather, to place them in the context of the larger socioeconomic and cultural settings from which they emerged.

The key to the power of the political machine was the ward heeler, the person who had a thoroughgoing knowledge of the ward. The ward heeler knew who needed a half ton of coal, who needed a job, who needed help with a hospital bill, or whose taxes were overdue, and so on. The ward heeler knew where the trade-offs were and where a bargain could be struck that would meet the needs of disparate parties and turn them into a coalition. All of these things, of course, meant votes and power.

I hope that I will not be misunderstood, at least initially, if I suggest that a pastor working with blue-collar people can view his or her role as a ward heeler. Obviously, certain characteristics of this role will have to be rejected on theological and ethical grounds but not those characteristics most important to fulfilling the pastoral task. The ward heeler image has at least three advantages. First, it is a role that can work in the complex relationships found in church and community. It has a proven record historically. Second, when properly conceived and practiced, it addresses the question of dignity in the relationships between pastors and working-class people. And finally, it is a way in which to build power with blue-collar people both in the church and in the community. I hope to demonstrate these advantages. To begin I need to delineate further what is meant by viewing the pastor as a ward heeler and to discuss certain dynamics of the role.

Quid Pro Quo

Reciprocity is a universal cultural norm. When one person helps another, the recipient has an obligation to return the favor. The arrangement is known as *quid pro quo,* "this for that." This norm can play an important part in building relationships where there were none before. One must face the fact that a good many pastors do not have strong ties to the larger blue-collar community. The pastor as ward heeler can use reciprocity to build strong ties to the blue-collar community.

Reciprocity begins with a pastor who looks for opportunities to do favors in the church and the community. Reciprocity and the doing of favors are understood by working-class people. While they are wary initially of people who try "to pull one over on them," they will recognize a genuine attempt to build relationship. They will accept the attempt when it is clear that the relationship is going to be equitable and not manipulative. That is, they know that a favor should be returned; they just want to be sure that the pastor does not get a lot more than what she or he gives. They do not want to be *used.*

Over the years blue-collar people have had "to make it" the best way they can. To do so, they know they need one another. Neighboring, helping one another out, doing and returning favors—these are key ingredients to working-class life. (It is, of course, not absent from the experience of all people.) For example, there is a "hidden economy" among working-class people in which not only do they buy and sell from each other, but also one person will help another "get a good buy" on an appliance or building materials, and so on. It is understood that these actions are favors; they are part of what it means to be a friend.

Ed Hill is a teamster and a friend of mine. Every time I buy something, he says, "Why didn't you talk to me first? I could've gotten that for you wholesale through this fellow I work with." When I say that I did not want to bother him, he says, "That's what friends are for."

I remember once that he replaced the engine and transmission in a '64 Plymouth of mine out of a Dodge his brother-in-law had given him. It was quite a job. I helped, ineptly; mostly I handed him wrenches. When I tried to pay him for his time, he refused. Later when he and Barbara got married, I did some premarital counseling and performed the wedding.

After we had had refreshments, Ed walked over to me and said, "Well, Tex, what do I owe you?"

I said, "Are you crazy, Ed? After all you've done for me, do you think I would accept money for this?"

"Aw, I knew you wouldn't take it. I just thought I'd better ask," he replied.

We both knew that I was returning a favor. I knew also that I still had not done as much for him as he had for me. I still owed him one—or two.

The Investment Model of Power

The ward-heeler role is a strategic way to build power and influence. In this role, power and influence are gained by doing favors. It can be thought of as an "investment model of power." That is, when one does someone a favor, one makes a "deposit" in one's account. It is a deposit one can "spend," a favor one can ask for in return. Two things need to be remembered. One is that deposits in an account tend to deteriorate and must be kept current; otherwise one runs the risk of someone asking, "So what have you done for me lately?" Second, one cannot spend influence one does not have; that is, one cannot operate out of a bankrupt account.

An illustration of this can be found when a pastor moves to a new church. Usually a deposit of influence is made in the pastor's account simply because the person *is* the new pastor. The honeymoon that pastors go through the first few weeks or months in a new church is constituted, in part, of this deposit. However, if the pastor does not soon—and very soon—begin to make deposits of her or his own through a wide range of acts of ministry, the honeymoon will come crashing down on the harsh realities of bankruptcy. By the same token, the pastor who provides services and does favors strengthens his or her position considerably.

By now, I dare say, some of you reading this are outraged by what may appear to be an outright subversion of the gospel and the nature and purpose of ministry. Reciprocity, quid pro quo, and an investment model of power seem thoroughly inconsistent with a gospel of grace in which the command to love is an imperative of Christian ministry, grace that prevails without regard to payoffs or benefits of any kind.

Let me try to say clearly what I mean. Reciprocity is a basic ingredient in blue-collar life-styles. It is understood differently by working-class people than by middle-class people because middle-class life operates on a different basis. The middle classes emerged at the end of the feudal period and had to make the case for their status on the basis of universal laws and civil rights. They claimed the right to own property as a basic human and civil right and opposed the divine right of kings in the name of more democratic institutions of government. This combination of values and group interests, proclaimed and sustained by the middle class, contributed mightily to the shape of the modern world. The political liberty that arose from this movement is, in my mind, the monumental contribution of bourgeois history.

The major beneficiary of this bourgeois contribution has also been the middle class. It is no secret that the laws of the Western world have been written on behalf of those who own property. And, except for more recent history when working-class people have owned their own homes, these laws have not benefitted them very much.

What this means is that universalistic notions of life and civil order are more characteristic of the middle class than of the working class. Universalisms often put blue-collar people at a disadvantage or leave them out altogether. For example, take the notion that the most academically talented youngsters should go on to college and receive aid because of their ability and promise. This is a reasonably sound, universalistic notion based on merit and potential contribution. Yet, abundant evidence suggests that I.Q. tests are class biased, that schools are far more responsive to middle-class and upper-class young people than to those who are blue collar and poor, and that college entrance exams reflect these same disadvantages for the working-class young. Blue-collar people know who is benefitted by high-sounding universalistic appeals, and they know it is not working-class people.[1]

So what does this have to do with the pastor as ward heeler? Simply this: the ward-heeler ministry style of doing favors is concrete, specific, and personal ministry. It is not talk; it is not a maze of ideas. The contract between giver and receiver is clear. Blue-collar people know that receiving a favor means returning a favor. The ministry that uses reciprocity operates on a basis that blue-collar people can recognize, understand, and trust.

Quid Pro Quo and Community

This next point is most important. For most blue-collar people, giving and receiving favors is not simply earning one's own way. Rather, giving and receiving favors is an expression of community. It is an expression of caring and friendship. It is not less than reciprocity, at least in ordinary circumstances; it is a good deal more. It is not merely contractual; in most instances it is the manifestation of covenant.

William F. May defines "contract" as "a circumstance in which two parties calculate their own best interests and agree upon some joint project in which both derive roughly equivalent benefits for goods contributed by each." What I like about the notion of "contract" is that it avoids what May calls "the conceit of philanthropy" and the "condescension of charity." It also

deals more directly with questions of power and control.[2]
However, as May points out, the

contractualist approach to professional behavior falls into the
opposite error of minimalism. It reduces everything to tit for
tat. . . . This kind of minimalism encouraged by a contractualist
understanding of the professional relationship produces a professional too grudging, too calculating, too lacking in spontaneity,
too quickly exhausted to go the second mile. . . .[3]

More important, a contract "suppresses the element of gift
in human relationships. . . ."[4] That is, from a Christian perspective it attempts to stifle the reality that we live out our
lives in an environment of grace. The pastor, as is the case
with any other professional or anyone else for that matter, has
not earned his or her way into life.

The indebtedness of a human being that makes his life—however
sacrificial—inescapably responsive cannot be fully appreciated by
totaling up the varying sacrifices and investments made by others
in his favor. Such sacrifices are there; and it is lacking in honesty
not to acknowledge them. But the sense that one is inexhaustibly
the object of gift presupposes a more transcendent source of do-
native activity than the sum of gifts received from others. For
the Biblical tradition this transcendent was the secret root of
every gift between human beings, of which the human order of
giving and receiving could only be a sign.[5]

A covenant is quite different from a contract. May points out
that the covenant between God and Israel included these basic
ingredients: the gift of Israel's liberation from Egypt, an exchange of promises, and the subsequent formation of Israel's
life by this promissory event.[6] This relationship became one in
which faithfulness exceeded any specification. If you will, covenant was the encompassing reality that included but was not
reducible to contractual agreement.

What I want most to convey is that a pastor *begins* a relationship with quid pro quo. The relationship does not end there.
The pastor begins with the giving of a gift, not from philan-
thropic heights, not in charitable condescension, and not in a
manipulative attempt to control but, rather, because he or she
stands in an environment of grace and wishes to signal a larger

covenantal reality, indeed to participate in the manifestation of this covenant in church and community. It may be that most blue-collar people do not articulate these relationships, but I believe without question that they sense and intuit them. The use of quid pro quo is one of the inchoate signs of community that include but are not reducible to reciprocity.

Several implications follow from this. First, the image of the power structure and influence is *not* that of a pyramid. Rather the image is that of a web, a web of transacted power and negotiated influence and control. This, after all, is the shape that power takes in genuine community. The image that the "bank account" of the pastor is full and that of church members and community people is empty or nearly so is not accurate here. Communal relationships are give-and-take.

Second, the pastor is to be a giver. When that giving is genuine and when it is concrete, specific, and personal, the pastor will be received into the community and its circle of loyalty.

Third, the pastor is to be a receiver. While some pastors make this too much of their ministry, other pastors simply resist receiving from others. Such a stance is not merely a strategic error; it imposes an indignity on working-class people.

I remember belonging to a youth group once in which several of the leaders were always doing *me* favors. Yet they never accepted any from me. I felt discounted, and I recognized after a time that these two or three leaders were able to exert enormous power over the group. Because I was young and did not know how to fight it, I withdrew.

The point is that pastors who cannot be receivers as well as givers place indignities upon blue-collar people because the giving and receiving of respect are out of balance. Moreover, I suspect, such a pastor is not owning up to a need for power that requires theological and ethical scrutiny. Some pastors feel so unworthy that they cannot accept gifts from God or a neighbor. Thus a need for power may grow out of a special kind of "works" righteousness in a person who has not accepted the Good News of God's grace in this important dimension of the self. Such a circumstance makes a bad witness of the reality of grace. The pastor who cannot receive offers a confusing testimony to people encouraged to accept and trust the gift of God's grace.

Fourth, in the trade-offs that occur some things clearly cannot be for sale or trade. At least two things can be suggested. One is the pastor's integrity. That cannot be traded away if the pastor wants to stay in a relationship of loyalty and community. Most important, the gospel cannot be traded away in the quid pro quo of reciprocity. The Good News of God's grace is the source and the aim of community. To sell this out is to lose the grounding of community and the key alternative to winner religion.

Finally, in the ward-heeler role one thing cannot be withheld—whether there is reciprocity or not—and that is love. Whether the love is returned or not, Christian faithfulness requires that it be offered again and again. We are not allowed to love only those who love us or to do favors only for those who return them. To be sure, sometimes love will need to be tough love, but that is love, nonetheless. Love cannot be withheld in the name of quid pro quo.

Ethnic Politics

The pastor as ward heeler operates with a political style that Andrew Greeley has termed "ethnic politics."[7] It is emphatically not the style of the intellectual; ethnic politics is

not given to articulating abstract ideas. . . . [rather it] is concrete and instinctual. Any attempt to state their model of the political process in formal terms—such as I will shortly engage in—is bound to lose something of the vigor and flavor of the original. On the other hand, while intellectual types may find the poor diction and malapropisms of some of the ethnic politicians vastly amusing, their amusement should not blind them to the fact that the best of politicians have an intuitive grasp of the city that would make the most skillful social scientist look naive.

The first assumption of ethnic politics is that the city is composed of various groups—national, racial, economic, religious.[8]

I want to point out that the church and the immediate community around it reflect some of this same diversity and plurality. In this setting it is the responsibility of the pastor as ward heeler to operate as a broker among the various groups.

It is the politician's role to act as a broker among these groups, arranging and rearranging power and resources in such a way as to prevent one group from becoming so unhappy with the balance that they will leave the system. He arranges, usually indirectly and informally, and almost always gradually, compromises among the various power elements within the city which these elements could not achieve by direct negotiations among themselves.[9]

Such political work is done without great fanfare, especially when change is accomplished. Moreover, it attempts to make sure that all groups are represented and that a consensus is built from which no major group is excluded.

This model of strategy is not a strategy for ideologues. Most people—especially blue-collar people—are not interested in ideology. Their concerns are more concrete: getting a job, being heard by a governmental bureaucracy, or receiving a service from a community agency or the church. This, of course, is an ideology of sorts, but it is a pragmatic one. It works on the basis of what is possible and seeks to satisfy as many groups as it can on the basis of what they want.

Ethnic politics is patronage politics. Hardly anything throws middle-class people into a tizzy faster than patronage. It is seen to be the very source of political corruption; it is vile. However, when government policy encourages a good business climate, offers tax inducements to business and professional people, and provides tax-free expense accounts, these are called "incentives."

Interestingly enough, however, Greeley maintains that it is not finally patronage that holds ethnic political organizations together. Loyalty is more important than pay-offs, and loyalty is what keeps people together. "As one young Irish lawyer put it, 'A man who is not loyal to his friends will never be loyal to an idea.'" Such loyalty requires one to "stand by your own."[10] This loyalty—even when twisted into corrupt forms—is a manifestation of the covenantal reality discussed previously.

Such a stance is difficult for middle-class people, especially liberals, to understand. It is one reason liberals have had so little effectiveness with working-class people. Liberals like ideas, especially theirs. Because of the nature of their middle-class, often professional, jobs they are geographically mobile and do not typically have deep communal ties. Hence the loyalty of ethnic politics escapes them and they dismiss it as "redneck," "hard hat," or lower-class "tribalism."

Ethnic politics has faults. High flexibility, a compromise orientation, and commitment to get people what they want (at least some of it) characterize its mode of operation. These characteristics make it prone to corruption, perhaps more so than "reform" models of politics. But reform models have more typically represented the business interests of a community than its working-class people or poor, and political models certainly have no corner on corruption in city politics.

Andrew Greeley has called attention to three critical weaknesses in ethnic politics. First, the responsiveness of ethnic politics to groups depends upon how well organized and articulate a given group is. Practitioners of this political model do not usually assist groups that need help in organizing and promoting their own interests. Second, the political model may overlook "small but potentially explosive groups." The experience Mayor Richard Daley had with the youth culture at the '68 Democratic Convention illustrates the reason for this. Greeley maintains that the Daley machine had had no experience with the youth and was unprepared to deal with them. "It learned quickly, and there has been no repetition of the [riot] scene in front of the Conrad Hilton, but the mistake of playing into the hands of the radicals was a function of the fact that until the convention, youth culture was not seen as a serious problem to cope with." Third, the intuitive, concrete style of the political strategist fails to communicate adequately with the intellectual, thus losing the contribution the intellectual can make in assessing long-range trends, which could complement the versatility of the political strategist in brokering more immediate demands.[11]

These weaknesses can be addressed by a trusted pastor. Working with people who can organize themselves and relating to "small, but potentially explosive groups," the pastor can function as an advocate and a go-between among groups in a neighborhood or suburban area. The pastor can work actively here, on a smaller scale, as a broker and interpreter. Because he or she has contacts with people outside the neighborhood or area, the pastor can groom relationships with planners, intellectuals, and agency people. When Richard Seaton led his church through the "End of Summer Festival," he found that this effort brought a lot of people together who did not know one another, and three organizations emerged from the gathering.

The ethnic politics approach is important in terms of the complexity of the local church. As I have shown, blue-collar people participate in churches with middle-class and upper-class persons. In pluralistic settings the role demands on a pastor to broker the claims and counterclaims of such groups are immense. When I have talked with knowledgeable pastors about quid pro quo and the substance of ethnic politics, I may have provided the name or concept, but they have experienced exactly what I am talking about. They have dealt with the situation for years. Their comments are typically, "Well, of course, you have to do that just to respond to the variety of people and needs in your congregation."

At this point one may wonder if local pastors are being encouraged to become political bosses. This is not my intention. Rather, I am asking pastors to look at the ward-heeler role and ethnic politics to gain from them the stylistic and substantive cues and directions for working with blue-collar people in both the church and the community. It is my conviction that whether the pastor wants to consolidate and conserve certain values and gains or wants to participate in social change with blue-collar people, these goals can most effectively be achieved through quid pro quo and a style of action akin to ethnic politics.

Knowing the Community

The pastor as ward heeler has to know the community. Back when I first moved to Kansas City, Missouri, a political machine was active in the blue-collar section of the city where I lived. A group of us liberals decided that we would get into the political fray and support a candidate who was challenging the boss politician of the area.

The machine had a candidate who held a patronage job but really did not seem to do much. Mainly he stumbled around the community talking to people in businesses, barber shops, bowling alleys, and the like. To us he looked as though he had all the sensibilities of a slab of beef. I thought to myself that if he represented the quality of organization the machine had, we would beat it hands down.

Let me tell you how wrong we were. In the election we got killed. We were beaten badly for a simple reason. That ward heeler could tell a person which square of sidewalk was cracked on any street in the ward. He knew everyone because he was constantly in conversation with people. He knew who was sick, who was retiring, who needed help. What he constantly did was find ways to help people. To be sure, it was quid pro quo; he wanted people's votes when the polls opened. It was understood that if he did someone a favor, that person owed him a favor. More than that, he had built a tremendous bond of loyalty between himself and the people of the ward.

Such an approach, theologically grounded, is a powerful one for pastors in blue-collar communities. To develop such knowledge of the community requires at least four basic orientations. The first is a street orientation—knowing people in the barber shops, the stores, the bars, the beauty shops, and the service stations. Visiting these places and others is requisite for getting in touch with blue-collar people, especially those who do not come to church.

The second orientation needed for intimate knowledge of a blue-collar community is seeing the neighborhood as the center of meaning and value for working-class people. Knowledge of the neighborhood's boundaries, of the relationships of people and groups within it, and of its needs and problems compose basic ingredients of this orientation. While the pastor may have more cosmopolitan interests and contacts, she or he must first see the neighborhood as *the* locality of action and contact in order to relate to working-class people. It is often the location of extended family relationships and close friends. Their homes are here and their house often is the only substantive wealth some blue-collar people ever own. Some middle-class professionals find it difficult to understand just how important the neighborhood is, but their effectiveness in working with blue collarites depends profoundly upon such an orientation.

Third, intimate knowledge of a blue-collar community requires an ethnic orientation. When the pastor appreciates both the diversity and the richness of American ethnicity, the ward-heeler pastor has a good "feel" for the different communities and knows how "to talk their language." A host of subtle skills are required to notice differences of etiquette, to catch nuances of meaning, to know what to say and do at a funeral or a wedding. The ward-heeler pastor will know the words that attract and relate and those that repel, will understand that one can sometimes talk too much and at other times too little. An intuitive grasp of moral sensibilities is necessary—knowing the jokes one *can* tell and those one cannot and *where* one can and cannot tell them. The subtleties of praise and insult are important dimensions of relationships and vary by ethnic group. There are also differences in approach to various age groups. If this style seems chameleonlike, it is because the pastor works in a complexity of ethnic colorings, seeking to appreciate and respond to a bright mosaic of diversity rather than a dull gray of ethnic imperialism.

Fourth, the ward heeler who wants to understand a blue-collar community needs a family orientation. Knowledge of the families and of the extended family relationships in the community may be essential to understanding some conflicts and ongoing feuds and may clarify the basis of long-standing coalitions and cooperating groups. Blue-collar people tend to do more socializing within extended family relationships than do middle-class people; thus knowledge of these relationships provides an awareness of community dynamics hardly available anywhere else. Not only is such knowledge important for understanding blue-collar communities but it is also crucial for strategic access to groups and as a tactical resource for moving and working in the community. For example, building coalitions for community action may be directly dependent upon one's ability to reach certain persons and groups through kinship ties. Moreover, the brokering of favors and services in the context of extended family relationships can be the key to a community problem.

What about pastors who live in suburbs, cities, towns, or rural areas that are not exclusively blue collar? Such a pastor simply needs to know where working-class people spend their time and needs to spend time there also in order to develop relationships. Such blue-collar hangouts would be cafes, taverns, bars, bowling alleys, barber shops, beauty shops, service stations, and car and motorcycle repair establishments. The pastor who knows the bar keepers, the beauticians, the barbers, and the other servicers of blue-collar hangouts will have his or her fingers on the pulse of that community.

Finally, the role of ward heeler will give a pastor the best access to the unchurched working-class people of a community. Knowing the community, going where a pastor is not expected, helping people simply because they have need, a pastor will be respected. This is true of other religious professionals as well.

One warm afternoon Ma Brown, a woman with nine children, told me in detail why the church was no good.

"Well, what about Marcia? She's the church. Does she help?" I asked. Marcia Johnson was a church and community worker who had been in that blue-collar community for ten years at the time. Marcia poured out her life for the people there.

"Marcia's different," Ma Brown immediately responded. "She's my church."

It is, finally, the people like Marcia, who do the favors, pay the price, and understand ethnic politics, who can reach the unchurched people in a community.

In sum, the pastor who wants to relate to blue-collar people will be profoundly instructed by the image of the ward heeler and the quid pro quo tactics and approaches to community life. Moreover, these are not inconsistent with Christian faith and ethics but indeed are means to express a profound loving concern, to seek and express community with working-class people, and to attempt deeper relationship through greater understanding. The pastor as ward heeler attempts to cast off middle-class imperialism in order to break down and cross dividing walls of hostility. Where he or she is effective, perhaps the ward *heeler* can become a ward *healer* as well.

Part IV

Community Organization and the Blue-Collar American

11

The Blue-Collar American and Community Organization

So far I have looked at a response by the church to blue-collar members and at a role for the pastor in the church and in the community. As important as these efforts are, it is clear that the church, no matter how effective its members and pastors may be, is not adequate by itself to meet the challenges posed by winner religion and the power distributions of American society. The ideology of achievement and structured social inequality are wedded at the depths of the structure and culture of the United States. Changes at this level are the most radical and the most difficult to accomplish. So far I have not addressed these larger issues. The role of the church, in my analysis, does not yet connect with the larger secular and national changes that are required. Two things are needed, especially at the local level: a new consciousness and the empowerment of working-class people.

Americans are committed to what Beth E. Vanfossen has described as *competitive class* consciousness, the belief that persons' "life chances depend on their own personal effort and resources in competition with other individuals in the society. . . ."[1] This is the religion of winning. In contrast, a *cor-*

porate class consciousness exists when "individuals believe that their own life chances depend on the actions and success of the class as a whole with which they identify."[2]

After a review of the research on class consciousness in the United States, Vanfossen concludes that about a fifth of the American people "either do not know what classes are or deny their existence."[3] Still she claims "that subjective social class is correlated with objective socioeconomic status (occupation in particular)." Even so, the "significant fact . . . is that people tend to perceive these differences not so much as *class* differences, but as *individual* differences, resulting from luck or from the application of talent and will."[4]

The second thing needed is the empowerment of ordinary people at the local level. I have shown in Part I the role of power in inequality. The concentration of power in the primary sector of the economy and the growing power of government pose grave threats to the workaday American. There will be no justice in American society without a redistribution of this power. In my opinion the best hope of change for blue-collar Americans and others who share a similar destiny is through grass roots action that begins in the neighborhoods of the country and moves on to larger public issues. It would not abandon the local base but remain anchored in concrete, local concerns as a way of focusing and sustaining the capacity to move beyond them.

Such grass roots action is already under way in new political developments at the local level. Across the United States, community organizations are forming. These are important not only because of the direct action in which they engage to advance the claims of working-class people and lower middle-class people, but also because they are settings in which empowerment and a new consciousness are formed.

What Is Community Organizing and What Does It Do?

Mike Miller, who directs a San Francisco-based training school for community organizers and activists, has defined community organization as *"a process of working with people to assist them to develop powerful, democratically run, 'mass-based' organizations through which they can defend and advance their interests and values.*"[5]

"Mass-based" means that large-scale participation by the membership governs the organization and its actions through democratic procedures and processes.[6] This mass-based governance is typically done first through the creation of a temporary neighborhood council, which is replaced as soon as possible by a more permanent organization. The council is really an organization of organizations, that is, organizers attempt to get *every* organization in the community to join and send representatives to the council. To get the participation of residential people who may not be members of organizations, block clubs are formed. The basic idea is to get as many people into the membership as possible and to do so by their participation in a group that belongs to the larger community organization.

Community organization is an exercise in empowerment which recognizes that most injustices are rooted in the fact that it is not in the self-interest of the powerful to change them. The powerful will not change unless confronted by power, and the way that working-class people can get such power is through organizing. The moral foundation of community organization is based on the principle that people have a right to participate in the decisions that affect them. As long as they are powerless, they will be denied this basic, human right.

Participation in community organizations has had a salutary effect on the hidden injuries of class, the subjective feelings of alienation, loss of dignity, and sense of failure. As we shall see later, participation in the struggle and action of an organization can have a transforming effect on people.

Community organization has been effective with poor people and blue collarites primarily because it begins with situations in their self-interest. That is, it attempts to organize a community by dealing with issues that are concrete, immediate, specific, and have some chance of being accomplished. Some of these issues are: getting a traffic light on a dangerous intersection, attacking redlining by banks, getting jobs for residents in companies located in the neighborhood or whose products are sold in the community, and the like.

This last point about choosing issues in which a victory is possible is a key point because the value of organizing for power has to be demonstrated. People in the lower end of the class structure have had too much experience with promises that are not fulfilled and with big ideas that do not change things. These victories become the stepping-stones to a greater competence in dealing with issues and in breaking the vicious cycles of failure and despair. When victories are achieved corporately, a deeper sense of self and community result.

Mike Miller has laid out the markings of an effective community organization. At the end of three to five years a community organization should at least:

—be actively defending and advancing the interests and values of the people it represents;

—have a democratic structure, with large-scale participation of the community in making basic policy decisions, electing leaders, and determining the basic governing rules of the organization;

—be self-funding through a combination of dues and fundraisers planned and implemented by the people themselves so that the core budget of $50,000 to $150,000 is paid for by the people themselves;

—have a list of victories on issues of concern to the people, who now act with confidence and competence when they deal with politicians, bureaucrats or businesspeople whose decisions might affect the lives of the people of the community;

—have expanded the horizons of local leaders so that they see the interrelationship of issues in their community as well as the relationship between problems in their community and broader decision-making or power structures;

—have developed among the people an appreciation and understanding of the values and procedures of democracy.[7]

Recent Developments in Community Organization

Community organizing received a great deal of media attention in the sixties, so much so that it is not really "in" anymore. In fact, it is possible to live in this country and not know about a vast array of organizations doing effective work. Community organization may be passé as a media event; yet it is still an effective tool of empowerment.

The method is especially effective with blue-collar people. This effectiveness grows, in part, out of changes that have come about since the sixties, which may be one of the reasons that the method no longer gets much media attention.

The sixties set the stage for grass roots action. The social movements of that period raised sharp national issues and mobilized people around them. Civil rights, welfare rights, the antiwar movement, the women's movement, the consumer and environmental movements raised questions of liberation, social justice, and peace.

The problem was, as Janice Perlman has observed, "when the smoke and commotion cleared and the TV cameras went away, people were left as anomic individuals relating symbolically to a national-level thrust."[8] What became clear after the sixties was put well by Richard Flacks: most people are less concerned with "making history than making life."[9] By and large, people simply do not remain mobilized for very long, especially if the issues are distant from their day-to-day lives. This is even more true for blue-collar people.

The result has been that effective community organizations since the sixties have focused "on local organizations and on issues which are more rooted in people's daily lives, have a longer-term perspective, and raise people's consciousness through involvement at a concrete level in their communities."[10]

Another development in community organizing is the need to build on a broad base rather than on a minority base only. For example, organizing only blacks typically pits them against the white working class who usually reside nearby with the consequence that the two groups become embattled and their common interests are lost. Effective community organizations are those that build on a multiracial basis.

Building community organizations on a broad base also means working with low- and moderate-income people. This makes possible organizations of poor people, working-class people, and moderate-income middle-class people. Some transitional and suburban churches that are pluralistic in membership are composed of the broad-based clientele needed by new forms of community organization. The churches, then, can work in such organizations.

A third development in community organizing is in ideology. The radical and conceptual rhetoric of the sixties has moderated so that the language now is more congruent with that of the people being organized and so that the ideology more accurately reflects where *people* are. Anyone who has been around blue-collar people at all knows how quickly—and sometimes irreversibly—they can be turned off by revolutionary "hot dogs." Note, for example, the deep and angry rejection of the student movement by blue-collar workers in the sixties and early seventies. In her assessment of community organizations in the seventies Perlman states:

> The groups now are for the most part strongly anticorporate, though not altogether anticapitalist. They are reformist more than revolutionary. Many in fact are dogmatically anti-ideological. Others consider themselves pluralist, populist, or progressive. Many of the leaders consider themselves radical, independent left, or even socialist, but they are so committed to consciousness through experience that they are often unwilling even to discuss their ideology in the abstract.[11]

For most people in the churches this change in rhetoric is crucial. Most church people, especially most blue-collar church people, will not be moved by radical rhetoric.

A fifth development is a growing diversity and eclecticism in community organizations. While the new organizations draw heavily on the kind of organizing advocated and practiced by Saul Alinsky since the fifties, their styles are also more mixed.

> They draw on union models, Cesar Chavez boycott models, welfare rights models, civil rights models, service provision, economic development, electoral involvement, etc. and invent new approaches as well as adopt pieces of others. What they all have in common is that they are independent community-based membership organizations (or coalitions of such organizations) composed of people acting on their own behalf. ... They deal in collective rather than individual activities and are typically both multi-issue and multistrategy groups.[12]

Finally, one weakness of community organization in the past

had been a too exclusive local focus. The efforts did not move beyond the neighborhood or community to broader issues. Harry C. Boyte recently surveyed community organization and citizen action across the United States. He found that community organization is moving into a number of different settings. Community organization of neighborhoods is vital and strong, but increasingly such organizations are taking on public-interest advocacy, such as that originally begun by Ralph Nader. Some community organizations are doing constituency organizing around issues that vary from consumer issues to anti-nuclear issues to boycotts of certain companies' products. Other organizations are deeply involved in electoral politics. Yet still others are involved in community-controlled and neighborhood-owned economic ventures. Some of these organizations are working on a citywide and statewide basis. Boyte sees in all this the beginning of a broad-based, national citizen movement. It demonstrates that community organization can move beyond neighborhood settings.[13]

A good illustration of such organizations is Massachusetts Fair Share. It is "one of the largest and most visible of a network of citizen action groups now organized in more than half the country's states."[14] Originally formed in 1975 from several community organizations in the Boston area, it works on neighborhood issues such as redlining, street repairs, and housing rehabilitation, and on larger public issues such as increased car insurance rates and utility costs.

> Fair Share is . . . a new kind of organization that fuses several traditions of organizing and public interest advocacy. Though its base is in communities, its programs are often divorced from any geographic definition of constituency. It has both at-large members and participants in community chapters. It gets most of its funds from door-to-door solicitation of the general public. And Fair Share has proven an effective tool for addressing issues in the broad "public interest."[15]

Moreover, Fair Share has built alliances between blacks and working-class whites, even in the aftermath of a bitter fight over busing.

Such organizing requires careful attention to local issues,

common interests, and the larger public interest. In these new types of organizations, all three must be kept strong. The biggest failure Fair Share had, according to Boyte, was when it took as a cause the disparity between electric rates for large industrial customers and residential users. On this issue there were "exaggerated tendencies toward staff control" in Fair Share, and the effort was not adequately rooted in the community. Even so, Fair Share was stronger in the contest, because of the neighborhood work that was going on at the same time, than many observers believed it would be.[16]

Community organization in the near future, if it is to address local issues and confront imbalances of power, will need to be locally based, publicly concerned, and organized around common interests that cross divisions of race, ethnic groups, and income levels.

Community Organization and Traditional Values

Community organization with blue-collar people requires an appreciation of traditional values, the values closest to the heart of working men and women: home, family, faith, neighborhood, and patriotism. These values are frequently derided by middle-class professionals, including religious ones.

Joe Holland has pointed out a basic difference between middle-class professionals and blue-collar people. The university training of the former *"tends to create an uprooted, highly individualized ego* [author's emphasis]." They move away from their homes and communities to go into the university, and from there middle-class professionals begin careers that carry them from place to place around the country. The result is that these professionals *find their source of identity and worth in a career.*[17]

In contrast, blue-collar people are far more likely to draw their identity *from the communities in which they live.* While variously secularized in the workaday world, they are most deeply committed to the traditional values of family, faith, and flag. These are particularistic values to cosmopolitan professionals, and these values receive more than a little sarcastic ridicule and demeaning abuse from university-trained people.

But middle-class professionals fail to understand the social origins of their own views and lack an adequate appreciation for those of working-class people. More than that, middle-class professionals fail to see the deeper significance of traditional values. In their haste to dismiss these values, they overlook the *meaning* the values have for working-class people.

Take patriotism, for example. No value of blue-collar Americans has perhaps been more sharply ridiculed. And let me say, the propensity to idolatry in patriotism requires critical vigilance. If one's focus, however, is only on the excessive misuses of a value, one misses its more healthy and appropriate meaning.

John Schaar has described the psychological bases of patriotism as "a whole way of being in the world captured best by the word *reverence,* which defines life by its debts: one is what one owes, what one acknowledges as a rightful debt or obligation."[18] Anyone who would understand the love blue-collar people have for their country must get in touch with this sense of indebtedness.

Moreover, that indebtedness is wedded to a sense of deep gratitude. The country, its people, its history, memories, customs are seen as precious gifts. To be patriotic is to acknowledge one's debts and to be grateful. To be sure, patriotism—like any other value—can become demonic, but this is a human problem not distinctive of working-class people only. And, parenthetically, a Christian point of view that lacks an appropriate love of country does not possess an adequate theology of culture.

Blue-collar people do not understand those who make fun of patriotism. Such ridicule is more than moral betrayal. It is *existential* betrayal because one is going against one's own roots and one's own sources as a human being.

The role that traditional values play in blue-collar life forces a rethinking of the standard right-wing and left-wing positions in the United States. Typically the left-wing position calls for the destruction of traditional values and the historical identities emerging from them so that an "emancipated consciousness" may come forth. "In the mainstream left, to be free means to be uprooted, detached from particularity, the new man or woman of socialist mythology."[19] The left tends to disparage traditional sources of identity such as the family, the church, voluntary associations, and ethnic background. These are the stagnant pools in which ignorance, bigotry, and superstition prevail. They are the spawning waters of capitalist values.[20]

On the other hand, conservatives tend to defend voluntary associations, traditional values, and institutions. They see home and family as the bulwark against encroachments of the power of the state. Seldom do they recognize the devastation of traditional values and institutions by a capitalist economy.

Thus an interesting similarity characterizes the basic theoretical positions of both left and right. Both see traditional values, institutions, and the identities arising from them as the foundation of the status quo. The crumbling of these traditional foundations would introduce unprecedented shifts. Consequently, conservatives defend these values and institutions as a way to resist change and to resist the power of the state, while radicals expect and hope for their demise as a way of promoting change.[21]

Both views are abstractions. In real life it is exactly in traditional groups of support, resources, and experience that people find the strength and the inspiration to change. Boyte poses the question pointedly: "Where do ordinary people, steeped in lifelong experiences of humiliation and self-doubt, barred from acquisition of basic public skills, gain the courage, the self-confidence, the mutual trust, above all the hope to take action in their own behalf?" Boyte believes that traditional values and institutions can be sources of significant change. Indeed, when these relatively autonomous institutions and organizations become energized in new ways and connected to networks of action beyond the local level, then people "develop the self-consciousness, skills, knowledge, and confidence to challenge those in control of their destinies."[22]

Blue-collar people are not abstractions, and they cannot be yanked from their cultural moorings. Rather, in the midst of these traditional values and institutions are resources and themes for making change, for insurgency, for revolt. Richard Flacks describes the pattern of social movements: "Most commonly, popular movements arise as efforts to resist threats to established patterns of everyday life." Such movements are most likely to occur when people believe those in authority are responsible for these threats.[23]

It is not my contention here to identify a middle ground between left and right. Quite frankly, such moderate positions strike me as irrelevant to the issues of the day. Rather I am posing an approach that begins locally but does not end there, that seeks to find the themes, sources, and support for change in certain traditional values and institutions and through them makes an assault on the dominant ideology and structures of power in contemporary society. Such a direction requires a reassessment and appreciation of traditional blue-collar values and institutions and a willingness to reorient oneself as a pastor or other religious professional.

By the same token, I have no desire to make an idol out of the nation and to encourage superpatriotism. If one sees blue-collar patriotism, however, as a sense of *indebtedness* for all that one has been *given,* one has a very different understanding with which to work. Such a sense of indebtedness brings its own themes and resources for change. It brings a sense of responsibility for the nation, an urge to take care of it in accord with the best of its traditions and with a renewed sense of the importance of ordinary people participating more directly in the issues that affect their lives.

To illustrate, a community organization composed of low-income residents of East Dallas called themselves the Bois d'Arc Patriots. They chose the name "Patriots" not only because the people in the neighborhood could relate to it but also because they wanted to designate their allegiance to the people, rather than allegiance to a government that did not represent them. They chose "Bois d'Arc" because it characterized the nature of their organizational commitment. Native to North Central and East Texas is the bois d'arc tree, one of the hardest and most durable woods of all North American trees. The wood was used by Native Americans to make long bows and by early white settlers to make plows. Bois d'arc trees were used to pave the first streets of Dallas, and many of the houses of East

Dallas still rest on bois d'arc foundations.[24] Such use of national, regional, and local symbols to call forth deep cultural meanings is hardly idolatry. The use of these symbols is a recognition of belonging and indebtedness, of who people are, and who they can become.

As I have shown, some blue-collar values are compensative; they attempt to make up for failing to make it to the top. So there is a fundamental conflict between the religion of winning and traditional blue-collar values like home, family, neighborhood, and country. For one thing the religion of winning does not have a profound sense of indebtedness and, if you will, reverence. Its individualism and competitiveness exalt a person for winning and blame a person for failing. If *I* have failed, I have no one else to blame. If *I* have won, I am not indebted. At the core of traditional blue-collar values is a sense of indebtedness.

This leads to the second point. Traditional blue-collar values are communal values. They stand in sharp contrast to the utilitarian strivings of achievement. Granted, in everyday life communal and utilitarian values are mixed, but it is an uneasy mixture because traditional blue-collar values draw their strength, in part, from a deep need to belong. Yankelovich has pointed out, "To be human is to belong, to be part of an entity larger than oneself—a family, a tribe, a neighborhood, a religion, an ethnic group, a social class, a profession, a society, a civilization."[25] In contrast, winning is far more individualistic. "The satisfactions of individualism come at an incalculable price, and a telling history of Western culture could be written around the theme of the dialectic conflict between individualism and belongingness."[26] While Yankelovich attempts to demonstrate on the basis of national surveys and interviews that "the shared meaning of respectability diminishes, and belongingness loses ground to individualism," nevertheless blue-collar people are among those who participate least in these shifts.[27] Moreover, Yankelovich concludes his study by suggesting that a new current is being struck in the culture in which a search has begun for belonging, for deeper and closer relationships, and for commitments that advance society as well as the self.[28]

The point is that traditional blue-collar values with their sense of indebtedness and the will to belong rest uneasily with the religion of winning. The consciousness raising that occurs in community organization offers an opportunity to split these two apart, and churches alert to the conflict between a gospel of grace and an achievement culture can provide new ways of defining and understanding life.

12

The Church and Community Organization

The church has been hobbled in its attempts to relate to blue-collar people by its stereotypes and lack of understanding. I have tried to present a picture of working-class people that appreciates their complexity and their humanity. I have also attempted to demonstrate that the church already has relationships with working-class people. They are *in* the churches. The job of the churches is to be more responsive, to develop a fellowship that is stylistically appealing and that presents the gospel in forms that communicate dignity by appreciation for blue-collar ways of relating to life and to the world. This is one part of the task to be done. It is not enough.

The blue-collar American is caught between two principalities and powers: winner religion and systemic imbalances of power. The concern of the last chapter was to look for an approach—effective in the local community—that could address these larger issues of ideology and power through new forms of consciousness and empowerment. That approach can be found in community organization, especially as it has taken shape in the seventies and early eighties. The purpose of this final chapter is to make the connection between the church

163

and community organization and to comment on a number of issues raised by this connection.

The Ward Heeler Pastor and Community Organizations

The pastor is obviously one of the most important persons for getting a church involved in community organization. His or her contact with church people and awareness of the politics within the congregation are crucial if the church is to become involved and stay active in a community organization.

Pastors are not usually organizers in community organizations, but by being ward heelers, as I have suggested, they have many opportunities to open doors to organizers and the organization, to assist in the formation of coalitions, to broker conflicts, and to give moral and theological legitimation to the rightful claims of people.

Warren Haggstrom, an authority on community organization, argues that "an organizer cannot follow a political organizational model since such models are developed solely to deliver votes by the politician doing things for people rather than by people doing things for themselves."[1] I agree that there is a difference between community organizations and political organizations and that the role of the organizer is different from that of a ward heeler, as I have defined it. However, I find his characterization of the political model "as developed solely to deliver votes" a highly reductionist description of what happens in ethnic politics. It fails to account for a great range of activities that take place in the relationship of a political organization to a community. These activities are reciprocal far beyond a mere delivery of votes. That this is so can be seen—if nowhere else—in the loyalty generated in ethnic politics and the symbolic role such organizations play.

Haggstrom's view also does not address the role that a ward heeler can play *in support* of a community organization. This supporting role is especially possible for a pastor who takes stylistic and strategic cues from the ward heeler and ethnic politics. The pastor's role is not usually that of organizer, but as ward heeler he or she can be one essential key in the development and work of the organization.

The pastor as ward heeler must identify with the people and make their cause truly his or her own. I looked hard for an example of a Protestant minister fulfilling this role since this book is aimed at Protestant churches. However, I could find no example as illuminating as the one which follows about a Catholic priest.

Identifying with the People

When Father Albert J. Benavides became pastor of St. Timothy Catholic Church in San Antonio, Texas, he encountered a parish membership that was 100 percent Mexican American with approximately 60 percent of its members falling below the United States poverty index. The remaining 40 percent were lower-class and middle-class civil service and maintenance workers. A third of the parish lived in housing projects subsidized by the government. The community was served by many social agencies and schools.

> As I became aware of all these facts and of all the facilities available I began to envision an alert, alive community coming together to care for its own needs. I found in time that this was not so. The schools & all the agencies in the parish had little to do with the people of the area; the people in fact did not feel much loyalty to them at all. The school taught their children, the agencies served those in need; and there the relationship ended. There was no involvement in the life of the people beyond giving the service expected.[2]

The one exception he found to this circumstance was the Catholic Church. "St. Timothy's was truly a neighborhood Center" and was the only institution to which people felt loyalty. Yet even at St. Timothy's there was dissatisfaction because the leadership core of the church wanted more say in running the church.

> They wanted to help formulate policy—not just consent to it. Another larger group of people felt alienated and disenchanted. They felt as if the church no longer cared about them, their culture, or their traditions. They came because they cared; but it was no longer a joyful experience.

Most of the people in the parish did not come to church at all. They felt no one cared for them or their views. Inadequate housing, high utility costs, watching their children walk to school through mud when it rained—these and other circumstances left them in a mood of "apathetic desperation."[3]

> They were saying that they were tired of having no say in their church or in their lives, they were tired of not having any control over their own destiny, they were tired of not having any options. I knew right away that if I were to have any success in reaching out to all of them, if I were to have any success in helping bring about a community of faith, hope, and love, the first reality that I would have to confront would be the people's powerlessness and the first place that I would have to begin would be the church.[4]

Father Benavides soon had his chance. A new church had been built in the parish in 1972 over the protests of the people. "It was a modern building that excluded many of the things the people felt comfortable with." In particular, a large crucifix, especially loved by the people, was not incorporated in the new building. The crucifix had been worked for, paid for, and installed by the people, but it was replaced in the new church with "an ultra-modern wrought iron crucifix," which was deeply resented. The people kept the old crucifix in their homes to make sure it was not lost.[5]

When Benavides arrived, he received hundreds of requests to place the old crucifix in the new church, but the architects and builders objected, contending that the old crucifix conflicted with the architectural lines of the church. Father Benavides, however, believed that people are more important than architecture; so he met with the leadership and "made plans for a large festival celebrating the return of the people's crucifix to their church."[6]

At a mass celebrated by the bishop, the original donor of the crucifix unveiled it before a crowd of nearly a thousand people. That did it. Father Benavides said:

> It was the beginning of my ministry there, for that event established the groundwork necessary for moving ahead; that event established the mutual acceptance so necessary for catechizing and evangelizing. It also indicated to me that one of the principal

catechetical arms of the community would have to be the liturgy.[7]

Father Benavides agrees with an observation by Virgil Elizondo that Spanish-speaking people are "sacramentalized but not catechized." Benavides maintains that, because of this, there is a "very intimate affinity between culture and sacramentalization."[8]

He felt, therefore, that "liturgy must reflect life as it is," and he saw that there was "little relationship between what happened inside the Church and what happened *outside* [author's emphasis]."[9]

What was needed was liturgy that dealt with the main issues of people's lives and that could combine celebration of life and commitment to improving the life God has given. Father Benavides began by integrating liturgy with prominent feasts and events. He began this experiment on Mexican Independence Day, a big day because Texas was a part of Mexico when it declared its independence from Spain.

> The first block of themes was therefore on Jesus Christ, the Liberator, the one who liberates us from sin which is the ultimate root of all injustice & oppression. The first week was spent reflecting on Jesus as a free man . . . [and on] the theme of liberation & liberty which is the nucleus of Jesus' message. We also developed the theme of oppression and people's response to it, & in developing this theme we utilized the Exodus event as exemplifying the process of a people going from oppression to freedom. This particular theme ended with the celebration of Dia de la Raza in which confluence and community are celebrated.[10]

At the same time Father Benavides gave attention to the great love of music and song in the Spanish-speaking community. He brought together seven musicians from the community and forty voices to form the choir, which later grew to fifteen musicians and almost a hundred voices.

Father Benavides then began to coordinate the teaching of the church and the church school with these liturgical and cultural themes. In the second year this liturgical-catechetical approach stressed the mission of the church and directly related the sacraments to the mission of the church: The sacraments were presented as "sacred moments in life" that assist each person to be liberated. This theme tied in with the 1976 celebration of the nation's Bicentennial. The theme and the year closed with a celebration of "liberty and justice for all."

The bringing together of Liturgy, Catechetics, and culture had indeed enhanced the caliber of our evangelization. Not only were we reaching more people but we were also reaching them more intensely and effectively.

In the meantime, those who actually ran the program were developing as leaders who took their place with the leadership core-group of the community. As more people became active leaders in one way or another, we greatly enhanced the ability of our parish to reach out to people.[11]

Yet Father Benavides and the leaders of the parish still felt "a disturbing anxiety" because they felt they were not doing enough. "We would talk about and celebrate the life & freedom that Jesus has given us knowing that things in the neighborhood would preach the opposite." People knew they were not really in charge of their destinies when they went from church to their homes, jobs, and schools.[12]

The church leadership realized that they would have to address the problems of the community, that they would have to identify with the struggle of the community and not with those of the church only. The first thing they did was to go to the people of the community to discover what was bothering them. They found that people were troubled most by poor streets, the lack of sidewalks, and the absence of parks for their children.

They held a series of meetings with at least two hundred and fifty people in attendance. After several meetings they decided on a ten-acre, city-owned vacant lot in front of the church as the site for the new park. Yet the people were fearful they could not get city hall to agree to their plan. However, after another series of meetings with city officials—this time attended by at least five hundred community people—they acquired the park and the necessary funding to develop it. Two months later they celebrated the groundbreaking. They began with a Mass of Thanksgiving and then walked to the park site where the groundbreaking took place.

This was the first of many community issues to be addressed, but Father Benavides and his parish did not do this work alone. When they decided to take on the needs of the community, several other parish communities were reaching the same decision. A number of churches came together to form "a citizen based organization that would address the capital & social needs of our people."[13] The churches collected money from six religious denominations, hired an organizer, and after a year of groundwork established Communities Organized for Public Service (COPS), a citywide organization that used the parish church as the basic building unit. Their first convention was attended by forty parishes and two thousand people. The second convention attracted four thousand people, and the third six thousand. In the first three years they brought close to $100 million in capital improvements to the community.[14]

Father Benavides concludes:

> While the experiences narrated could never be duplicated anywhere, the principles underlying them are valid and important. Before people can respond . . . to the mystery of Christ, before people can experience the fulfilling process of conversion, there must be established between people & church a relationship that is built on acceptance and trust. This acceptance and trust can flow only from a deep & firm respect—respect for who people are, their traditions & customs, their culture, and above all their struggles. In my parish, that acceptance & trust was established through a respectful concern for the symbols of the people. Only then were we able to talk of the vital issues confronting the community.[15]

COPS under the leadership of people like Father Benavides and Ernie Cortes, an outstanding organizer, became the largest community organization in the United States. Its strength resided in its capacity to continue to work with local nitty-gritty issues and, at the same time, to address broader questions. It got streets repaired, but it also had a profound effect on electoral politics. No little reason for its effectiveness has been the churches and their leaders who have identified with the people, relating faith to their culture, tradition, and struggle.

However, the experience of St. Timothy and the other churches in COPS does raise an important issue currently debated in community organizing. The approach that worked in San Antonio may not work everywhere.

Constituency Organizing Versus Institutional Organizing

Saul Alinsky's approach to community organization was to build an organization of organizations. In San Antonio this meant that churches, businesses, voluntary associations, block clubs and so on were sought out to be members and each member then sent representatives to conventions and other meetings and actions of the community organization. For Alinsky churches were key organizations, and he argued that the larger organization should be built on them.

In the early 1950s Fred Ross, an Alinsky co-worker, began to take exception to this idea. He contended that if an organization is to move beyond the neighborhood, if it is to operate throughout an entire region, it must win the support of the churches but need not rest upon them. In an alternative approach he used house meetings to discuss issues of importance to working-class people. With this approach he organized the Community Service Organization in the Mexican-American community of the southwest in the late 1950s. Ross's approach influenced the farm worker organizing of Cesar Chavez, the National Welfare Rights Organization and the new "majority strategy" of the seventies.

This difference in approach between Alinsky and Ross led to two traditions in community organization with the result, as Harry C. Boyte notes, that "A hard choice faces any major organizing project: whether to concentrate on mobilizing a broad constituency . . . or whether to involve, build upon, and transform existing community institutions."[14]

This debate clearly has important implications for the church. In the traditional Alinsky approach, as in San Antonio, the churches are key organizations. In Ross's approach churches are supportive and have a role, but not a key one.

I think there are basically two responses to this choice. One of them involves local cultural patterns. It is difficult to imagine building an organization like COPS in San Antonio without involving the churches, especially the Roman Catholic Church. The same would be true in many communities of white ethnics on the East Coast. I cannot imagine community organizations in South or Midwest communities that could be successful without involvement of Protestant churches. Involvement of the churches would be very important if one were attempting to organize blacks, given the central role played by the church in the black community.

"In contrast," Boyte suggests, "in the glass and steel ghettos of downtown skyscrapers, social networks are weak or nonexistent in the beginning of an organizing effort."[15] In these settings a constituency approach would seem to have the best chance of success, except that the situation is more complex than this.

Boyte points out that while constituency-based approaches in the 1970s had rapid growth and were effective in addressing the big issues, these approaches often led to conflict with other, older organizations and tended to take on larger issues "at the expense of basic problems close at hand."[16] In time this loses the local grounding necessary to keep the commitment of people around the issues that immediately concern them and to provide strength for the broader, more public issues. As noted in the previous chapter, community organization in the present needs to be strong in the local neighborhoods if it is to take on the bigger public issues. This is especially true for working-class Americans.

This leads to the second response. Constituency-based efforts need to be combined with institutional organization. In his study of the citizen action movement in the United States Boyte states:

The most effective organizations of the citizen revolt . . . have addressed such tendencies straightforwardly, showing that depth and attention to broader questions need not be antithetical. Furthermore, a number of organizers and groups out of the constituency tradition have begun to modify their approach. When Kim Clerc [an organizer] left the Citizens Action League in California to begin organizing in Oregon, the committee sponsoring Oregon Fair Share included churches, labor unions, and other groups. Similarly Massachusetts Fair Share has given increasing atten-

tion to the involvement of church groups and its new organizing
director, Stan Holt, comes out of a more traditional Alinskyite
approach. Groups like Ohio Public Interest Campaign and the
Illinois Public Action Council self-consciously build on both institutional and constituency traditions of organizing.[17]

The community organizations called for in our time need
both traditions, and the church continues to have an important
role in such efforts.

In local neighborhoods the church also has unusually good
ties with women. Women participate more actively in church
than do men, a fact that holds true for blue-collar women as
well.

Community Organizations and Women

One of the richest—and as yet relatively unrecognized—
resources for community organizations in the blue-collar community is women. One of the reasons for this lack of recognition
is the stereotype of such women, one advanced in no little part
by social science. Virginia McCourt sums up this stereotype:
a woman confined to the world of her family, her life centered
on being a housewife, raising her children, and taking care of
her husband. She does not belong to clubs or organizations and
has limited contact with the outside world. Her best friends
and guests are members of her own family. Television is her
mainstay against boredom and constitutes the companionship
and stimulation she gets beyond her relationship with family,
children, and husband.[18]

Doubtlessly this stereotype fits some blue-collar women.
However, one can recall the participation of working-class
women in labor strikes and neighborhood protests of the past.
It is more likely, argues McCourt, that the stereotype comes
from the period following World War II when women were
encouraged, as part of national duty, to return home so that
their veteran husbands could find jobs in the workaday world
and normalcy could return.[19]

This stereotype does not hold among women involved in what
McCourt calls "assertive community organizations." In her study
of southwest Chicago she found significant patterns of partic-

ipation by working-class women in grass roots community action. Her findings are informative for those who intend to work with blue-collar people, especially women, and for the role of the church.

McCourt wanted to know what led some women to become active in community organizations with an assertive political orientation. She found that the women most likely to become involved in the organizations were those who had heightened political awareness and anger. They saw conditions worsening and core institutions not responding to the conditions. Seeing these things led them to cynicism and despair which, interestingly enough, led them to believe that they could do something about the situation. Their opportunity for action came at the point of *being invited* into a community organization. These women were also likely to see women as victims of oppression. They had a strong attachment to the neighborhood and feared losing the sense of community they found there. Both of these latter characteristics may grow from involvement in community organizations.

The most involved women did not have a paying job outside the home or preschool children in the home. They had the minimal support of their husbands, and these husbands tended to have a high-school education or more. Finally, the parents *of the husbands* typically did not live in the immediate neighborhood, and so the women were not constrained by a tight family nexus. Parenthetically, the presence of the women's parents did not seem to have a constraining effect on the participation of the women in community organizations.

These characteristics of highly involved women become a checklist, if you will, of the best recruitment prospects for a community organization. Women with these characteristics are most open to involvement in community organization.

What is important for purposes here is McCourt's finding that the women most involved in community organizations were also involved in the church.

Some kind of affiliation with the school and, especially, with the church seems to be important. It is within the church and the school that basic values are taught and reaffirmed. The strong

bonds which exist among these neighbors, despite minimal visiting and social contact, are based on perceived similarities in
values and life style. The coming together at church and school
functions may provide the occasion for a reaffirmation of such
shared values and, in the absence of any other mechanism for
regular contact among neighbors, may be especially important.[20]

Here, again, the church has strategic access to a group of
people who are ready and willing, it seems, to become involved
in community organizations and to take action on behalf of
themselves, their families, their homes, and their communities.

Traditional Values and Women

I have defended the basic role that traditional values have
in organizing blue-collar communities. Yet many women will
raise questions about their own fate in an approach that works
within these values. Does working within traditional values
consign women to continuing subjugation? Several points need
to be made in answer to this question.

First, my conviction is that the *only* avenue of change that
has a real chance with blue-collar men and women is one that
draws on and is legitimated by traditional values. Second, an
appeal to traditional values does not *have* to mean business as
usual. Within traditional values are themes for reinterpreting
the role and status of women. As Flacks said, popular movements emerge in response to threats to established patterns of
everyday life. Such movements open up new options for women.

Their participation in community organizations leads women
to a new consciousness and a new role for themselves. Virginia
McCourt found that active participation in community organizations brought greater political consciousness and increased feelings of self-esteem and developed strong feelings
of community attachment. McCourt sees all of these changes
as "part of the role transformation that is occurring in the lives
of working class women" and that is broadening their experience and the social boundaries of their lives.[21]

It is clear, because of her own political commitments, that
McCourt hopes such a shift in attitudes might provide the basis
for a new populism. However, while the women in southwest

Chicago see their circumstances with increasing clarity, McCourt reports that "there is still a strong tendency to define [problems] in narrow, immediate, and easily remediable terms rather than to see them as one part of a political and economic system that operates counter to their interests."[22]

In a word, the women in McCourt's study are nonideological. They are realizing some of their interests at the local level, but there is little indication that their "exclusively local base and orientation" might dispose them to support a candidate at the national level or to question the social-class system itself. At best, McCourt reports, "there is a spirit within these groups that suggests an openness to new political demands and directions."[23]

This is the point at which the connection between local community organizations and constituency-based organization is so important. Such a connection relates local concerns to larger public issues. The relationship of institutional and constituency organizing—so crucial for a new, citizen-action movement—is equally significant for the transformation of blue-collar women.

Given the participation of blue-collar women in religious institutions, the churches have an important role to play. However, to play this role the church and its leadership will need to do some considerable changing of its own. Its gospel of grace will need to address the plight of women.

As the church and the pastor work with community organizations, two crucial issues will arise again and again, those of human dignity and power. A discussion of each of these will follow.

Grace and Dignity

Community organization can empower and change the consciousness of people. It can take people in their traditional lifestyles and settings and concentrate their power to address the common issues that face them. Community organization can be the situation in which people find a renewed sense of dignity and hope. Bill Talcott, a community organizer, described his work to Studs Terkel:

You must listen to them and tell them again and again they are important, that they have the stuff to do the job. They don't have to shuck themselves about not being good enough, not worthy. Most people were raised to think they are not worthy.[24]

Life-transforming experiences occur in the midst of such organizing and encouragement. Talcott reports one special and telling case.

In San Francisco, our organization licked the development agency there. We tied up two hundred million dollars of its money for two years, until [they] finally came to an agreement with the community people. The guy I started with was an alcoholic pimp in the black ghetto. He is now a Presbyterian minister and very highly respected."[25]

Here there is a convergence of the work of community organization and the church because community organization can be and often is a residence of grace. The message of community organization, in part, is to proclaim to people their worth and dignity. This is a message that undermines winner religion at its foundation.

Let me be clear: *community organization does not prove people's worth; it demonstrates it.* And the more that working-class people understand the role of winner religion in justifying inequalities, the more that the getting-giving compact shifts so that people no longer believe the rat race is worth it; the more that people seek to belong rather than to dominate, then the more deeply will they be creatively alienated from an ideology that oppresses them. The role of the church is to offer a nonsecular alternative, a gospel of grace as antidote to an achievement culture.

As all of this takes form in community organizations, the church will face again and again the issue of power and the rationale for the church's involvement in power struggles. How does the message of love relate to empowerment?

Love and Power

The thing that so many Christians and others fail to understand is that power is a fundamental human need. Paul Tillich's view suggests that without power, in an absolute sense, one cannot be at all.[26] But one does not have to place the issue in ontological terms to make the case for power as a need. Power is a fundamental human need because so many other needs depend upon it. One never sees a person with power who is involuntarily hungry or who lacks shelter or clothing or adequate medical care. These are the conditions of powerlessness, and there is finally no help for such persons without empowerment.

The good Samaritan story in Luke 10 gives the clear teaching that anyone in need is a neighbor and that the responsibility of a Christian is to answer the other's need. To respond to neighbors whose basic need is power requires a new orientation of life for most Christians because empowerment then takes on the same status as the cup of cool water for the thirsty, clothing for the naked, food for the hungry, sight for the blind. This is a new way of looking at release for the captives.

The question is: How can this be done? I agree with those who claim that power cannot be given. Power given to someone is power derived from someone else. It is too easily taken away. What is called for is not a gift of power but an identification with those without power, a taking of sides, and a willingness to struggle with and for the powerless. This involves vulnerability and risk. This is precisely what the church is called to do if it is to take seriously the empowerment of working-class people and poor people.

A Concluding Word

Blue-collar Americans are caught in a web of ideology and relative powerlessness. Winner religion sets us all in a futile contest for dignity, and working-class people find achievement myths blocked by the power imbalances of structured social inequality. This reality of losing leaves blue collarites in an ecology of encounters in which orders are taken, in which respect is given and not received, and in which blue collarites are haunted by the experience of failure. To be sure, some are better off than others, and we have seen the adaptive and compensatory life-styles of blue-collar winners, respectables, survivors, and hard livers.

Blue-collar religious expression has not responded adequately to competitive class consciousness and power imbalances that set the secular fate of working-class people. It is my conviction, however, that an authentic Christian faith can be incarnate in blue-collar religious form and participate in the empowerment of working-class people. It requires pastors who can see themselves as ward heelers, practicing a baptized ethnic politics in the context of an encompassing covenantal reality.

This alone, of course, cannot redress the inequities of America. Needed also are community organizations, based in the neighborhoods and local communities of the nation, that provide the foundation for large public networks of citizen action. In these the church has an important role to play. If the church cares about working-class people, if it cares about ordinary people all across this country, the time is ripe to get going.

Notes

Introduction

[1] Bob McDill, Wayland Holyfield, and Chuck Neese, "Rednecks, White Socks and Blue Ribbon Beer." Copyright Jack Music, Inc. and Jando Music, Inc. All Rights Reserved. Quoted in Frye Gaillard, *Watermelon Wine* (New York: St. Martin's Press Inc., 1978), p. 216.

[2] Peter Schrag, "The Forgotten American," *Harper's* (August, 1969), p. 27.

[3] Quoted in Philip Nobile, ed., *The Con III Controversy* (New York: Pocket Books, 1971), p. 219. Quoted by Daniel Yankelovich, *New Rules* (New York: Random House Inc., 1981), p. 34.

[4] Emile Pin, "Social Classes and Their Religious Approaches," *Religion, Culture and Society,* ed. Louis Schneider (New York: John Wiley & Sons Inc., 1964), p. 414.

[5] Lillian Rubin, *Worlds of Pain: Life in the Working Class Family* (New York: Basic Books, Inc., Publishers, 1976), p. 5.

[6] U.S. Bureau of the Census, *Money Income of Household, Families, and Persons in the United States: 1980,* pp. 126-127, 130-131.

Chapter 1

[1] Daniel Yankelovich, *New Rules* (New York: Random House Inc., 1981), p. 14.

[2] *Ibid.,* p. 8.

[3] *Ibid.,* p. 141.

[4] John C. Raines, *Illusions of Success* (Valley Forge: Judson Press, 1975), p. 77.

[5] Jean B. Miller, *Toward a New Psychology of Women* (Boston: Beacon Press, 1976), pp. 19-20.

[6] Raines, *Illusions*, p. 78.

[7] Beth E. Vanfossen, *The Structure of Social Inequality* (Boston: Little, Brown & Co., 1979), p. 239. Copyright © 1979 by Beth Ensminger Vanfossen. Reprinted by permission of Little, Brown, and Company.

[8] *Ibid.*, p. 241.

Chapter 2

[1] Robert W. Cox, "Labor and the Multinationals," *Foreign Affairs* (Jan., 1976) p. 345.

[2] *Ibid.*, p. 349.

[3] Barry Bluestone, William M. Murphy, and Marry Stevenson, *Low Wages and the Working Poor* (Ann Arbor: University of Michigan Institute of Labor and Industrial Relations, 1973), pp. 28-29. Quoted in E. M. Beck, Patrick M. Horan, and Charles M. Tolbert II, "Stratification in a Dual Economy: A Sectorial Model of Earnings Determination," *American Sociological Review*, 43 (October, 1978), pp. 706-707.

[4] *Ibid.*, p. 707.

[5] Beck, *et al.*, "Stratification," p. 710.

[6] *Ibid.*, p. 714.

[7] *Ibid.*, p. 716.

[8] Beth E. Vanfossen, *The Structure of Social Inequality* (Boston: Little, Brown & Co., 1979), p. 129.

[9] *Ibid.*

[10] Delbert C. Miller and William H. Form, *Industrial Sociology: Work in Organizational Life*, 3rd. ed. (New York: Harper & Row, Publishers, Inc., 1979), p. 638.

[11] *Ibid.*

[12] *Ibid.*

[13] *Ibid.*, pp. 638-639.

[14] *Ibid.*, p. 639.

[15] *Ibid.*, pp. 639-640.

[16] *Ibid.*, p. 640.

[17] Vanfossen, *Structure*, p. 124.

[18] O. D. Duncan, "Inheritances of Poverty or Inheritance of Race?" *On Understanding Poverty: Perspectives from the Social Sciences*, ed. Daniel P. Moynihan (New York: Basic Books Inc., Publishers, 1968), p. 108. Quoted in Vanfossen, *Structure*, p. 125.

[19] Vanfossen, *Structure*, p. 125.

[20] Louise K. Howe, *Pink Collar Workers: Inside the World of Women's Work* (New York: G. P. Putnam's Sons, 1977), p. 7.

[21] Vanfossen, *Structure*, p. 126.

[22] *Ibid.*

[23] *Ibid.*, p. 131.

[24] H. M. Wachtel and Betsey, "Employment at Low Wages," *Review of Economics and Statistics*, 54 (1972), pp. 121-129. Quoted in Vanfossen, *Structure*, p. 131.

[25] Randall Collins, *Conflict Sociology* (New York: Academic Press Inc., 1975), pp. 418-421.

26 Barry Bluestone and Bennett Harrison, *The Deindustrialization of America* (New York: Basic Books Inc., Publishers, 1982). Quoted in Richard Gillett, "The Reshaping of Work: A Challenge to the Churches," *The Christian Century*, 100 (January 5-12, 1983), p. 11.
27 Richard Gillett, "The Reshaping of Work: A Challenge to the Churches," *The Christian Century*, 100 (January 5-12, 1983), p. 11.
28 *Ibid.*, p. 12.
29 *Ibid.*, p. 13.

Chapter 3

1 Randall Collins, *Conflict Sociology* (New York: Academic Press Inc., 1975), p. 156.
2 *Ibid.*, p. 54.
3 Melvin L. Kohn and Carmi Schooler, "Class, Occupation, and Orientation," *American Sociological Review*, 34 (October, 1969), p. 659.
4 *Ibid.*, p. 666.
5 *Ibid.*, p. 667.
6 *Ibid.*, pp. 667-669.
7 *Ibid.*, p. 671.
8 Susan E. Kennedy, *If All We Did Was to Weep at Home: History of White Working-Class Women in America*, Minorities in Modern America Series (Bloomington: Indiana University Press, 1979), p. 221.
9 Louise K. Howe, *Pink Collar Workers: Inside the World of Women's Work* (New York: G. P. Putnam's Sons, 1977), p. 31.
10 *Ibid.*, p. 38.
11 Mary Lindenstein Walshok, *Blue Collar Women* (New York: Doubleday/Anchor Press, 1981), p. 152. Copyright © 1981 by Mary Lindenstein Walshok. Reprinted by permission of Doubleday & Company, Inc.
12 *Ibid.*, p. 153.
13 Lillian Rubin, *Worlds of Pain: Life in the Working Class Family* (New York: Basic Books Inc., Publishers, 1976), p. 169.
14 Collins, *Conflict Sociology*, p. 111.
15 Elliott Liebow, *Tally's Corner: A Study of Negro Streetcorner Men* (Boston: Little, Brown & Co., 1967), pp. 61-62. Copyright © 1967 by Little, Brown and Company, Inc.
16 Howe, *Pink Collar Workers*, pp. 239-240.
17 Liebow, *Tally's Corner*, p. 221.
18 *Ibid.*, pp. 210-211.

Chapter 4

1 Wan Sang Han, "Two Conflicting Themes: Common Values Versus Class Differential Values," *American Sociological Review*, 34 (Oct., 1969), pp. 679-690.
2 E. E. LeMasters, *Blue Collar Aristocrats: Life Style at a Working Class Tavern* (Madison: University of Wisconsin Press, 1975), p. 20.
3 *Ibid.*, p. 25.
4 *Ibid.*, pp. 26-27.
5 *Ibid.*, p. 128.
6 *Ibid.*, p. 107.

[7] *Ibid.*, p. 46.
[8] *Ibid.*
[9] *Ibid.*, pp. 54-77.
[10] Mary Lindenstein Walshok, *Blue Collar Women*, (New York: Doubleday/ Anchor Press, 1981), p. 85.
[11] *Ibid.*
[12] *Ibid.*, p. 86.
[13] *Ibid.*, pp. 111-112.
[14] *Ibid.*, p. 115.
[15] *Ibid.*, p. 118.
[16] *Ibid.*, p. 132.
[17] *Ibid.*, p. 133.
[18] *Ibid.*, p. 134.
[19] *Ibid.*, p. 139.
[20] *Ibid.*
[21] *Ibid.*, pp. 14, 141-152.
[22] *Ibid.*, p. 206.
[23] *Ibid.*
[24] *Ibid.*, p. 255.

Chapter 5

[1] Richard Sennett and Jonathan Cobb, *The Hidden Injuries of Class* (New York: Random House Inc., 1972), pp. 26-27. Copyright © 1972 by Richard Sennett and Jonathan Cobb. Reprinted by permission of Alfred A. Knopf, Inc.
[2] Joseph T. Howell, *Hard Living on Clay Street* (New York: Doubleday/Anchor Books, 1973), p. 6. Copyright © 1973 by Joseph T. Howell. Reprinted by permission of Doubleday & Company, Inc.
[3] Cobb and Sennett, *The Hidden Injuries of Class*, p. 48.
[4] *Ibid.*, p. 49.
[5] Lillian B. Rubin, *Worlds of Pain: Life in the Working Class Family* (New York: Basic Books Inc., Publishers, 1976), p. 186.
[6] *Ibid.*, p. 188.
[7] Hank Williams, "Your Cheatin' Heart." Copyright © 1952 Fred Rose Music, Inc. All Rights Reserved.
[8] Rubin, *Worlds of Pain*, p. 36.
[9] Howell, *Hard Living on Clay Street*, p. 9.
[10] *Ibid.*, p. 308.
[11] *Ibid.*, p. 312.
[12] Daniel Yankelovich, *New Rules* (New York: Random House Inc., 1981) p. 111.
[13] *Ibid.*, pp. 111-112.
[14] *Ibid.*, p. 120.
[15] *Ibid.*, p. 117.
[16] *Ibid.*, p. 122.
[17] *Ibid.*, p. 88.
[18] *Ibid.*, p. 122.
[19] *Ibid.*, p. 132.

Chapter 6

[1] Joseph A. Kahl, *The American Class Structure* (New York: Holt, Rinehart & Winston General Book, 1957), pp. 205-210.

[2] *Ibid.*, pp. 205-206.

[3] Lillian B. Rubin, *Worlds of Pain: Life in the Working Class Family* (New York: Basic Books Inc., Publishers, 1976), p. 158.

[4] H. Roy Kaplan and Carlos E. Kruytobosch, "Sudden Riches and Work Behavior: A Behavioral Test of the Commitment to Work." Delivered at the Seventieth Annual Meeting of the American Sociological Association, San Francisco, California, August 25-29. Quoted in Rubin, *Worlds of Pain*, p. 234, n. 9.

[5] Susan E. Kennedy, *If All We Did Was to Weep at Home: A History of White Working-Class Women in America*, Minorities in Modern America Series (Bloomington: Indiana University Press, 1979), p. 232.

[6] Rubin, *Worlds of Pain*, p. 173.

[7] Kennedy, *If All We Did*, p. 229.

[8] Rubin, *Worlds of Pain*, pp. 185-203.

[9] Kahl, *The American Class Structure*, p. 209.

[10] Melvin L. Kohn and Carmi Schooler, "Occupational Experience and Psychological Functioning: An Assessment of Reciprocal Effects," *American Sociological Review*, 38 (February, 1973), p. 116.

[11] *Ibid.*, p. 117.

[12] Note: This finding of Kohn and Schooler flies in the face of Rubins's finding that men compensate for the lack of creativity in their jobs by working on projects at home. I have "solved" this question in my own mind in the assertion that they are talking about different groups of blue-collar men. Rubins's observation is more typical of respectables, and Kohn and Schooler are describing survivors.

[13] Quoted in *Work in America: Report of a Special Task Force to the Secretary of Health, Education and Welfare* (Cambridge, Mass.: M.I.T. Press, 1976), p. 186.

[14] Kahl, *The American Class Structure*, p. 208.

[15] Ely Chinoy, *Automobile Workers and the American Dream* (New York: Doubleday & Co., Inc., 1955), p. 82. For more recent support of this point see Rubin, *Worlds of Pain*, pp. 161-163.

Chapter 7

[1] Joseph T. Howell, *Hard Living on Clay Street* (New York: Doubleday/Anchor Press, 1973), p. 6.

[2] *Ibid.*, p. 267.

[3] *Ibid.*, p. 268.

[4] *Ibid.*, p. 273.

[5] *Ibid.*

[6] *Ibid.*, p. 274.

[7] *Ibid.*, p. 291.

[8] *Ibid.*, p. 277.

[9] *Ibid.*

[10] *Ibid.*, p. 291.

[11] *Ibid.*, p. 299.

[12]*Ibid.*, p. 303.
[13]*Ibid.*
[14]*Ibid.*
[15]*Ibid.*, p. 305.
[16]*Ibid.*
[17]*Ibid.*, p. 307.
[18]*Ibid.*
[19]*Ibid.*, p. 313.
[20]*Ibid.*, p. 326.
[21]*Ibid.*, p. 331.
[22]*Ibid.*, p. 332.
[23]*Ibid.*, p. 333.
[24]*Ibid.*, p. 337.
[25]*Ibid.*
[26]*Ibid.*, p. 340.
[27]*Ibid.*, p. 343.
[28]*Ibid.*, p. 346.
[29]*Ibid.*, p. 352.

Chapter 8

[1]J. Russell Hale, *The Unchurched: Who They Are and Why They Stay Away* (San Francisco: Harper & Row Publishers, Inc., 1980), p. 175. Cf. George Gallup, *Survey of the Unchurched American* (Princeton: Gallup Organization, 1978) and David A. Roozen, *The Churched and the Unchurched in America: A Comparative Profile* (Washington, D.C.: Glenmary Research Center, 1978).

[2]*Ibid.*, p. 175.

[3]Joseph T. Howell, *Hard Living on Clay Street* (New York: Doubleday/Anchor Press, 1973), pp. 141-142.

[4]These statements are my summary of attitudes and comments found in Howell's study. *Ibid.*, pp. 174-175, 209-210, 313-314.

[5]Robert S. Lynd and Helen M. Lynd, *Middletown* (New York: Harcourt Brace Jovanovich, 1929), p. 329.

[6]Yoshio Fukuyama, "The Major Dimensions of Church Membership," *Review of Religious Research*, 2, 4 (Spring, 1961), pp. 154ff; Rodney Stark, "The Economics of Piety: Religious Commitment and Social Class," *Issues in Social Inequality*, ed. Gerald D. Thielbar and Saul D. Feldman (Boston: Little, Brown & Co., 1972), pp. 483-503; Nicholas J. Demerath, III, "Social Stratification and Church Involvement: The Church-Sect Distinction Applied to Individual Participation," *Review of Religious Research*, 2, 4 (Spring, 1961), pp. 146-154.

[7]H. Paul Chalfant, Robert E. Beckley, and C. Eddie Palmer, *Religion in Contemporary Society* (Sherman Oaks, Calif.: Alfred Publishing Co., Inc., 1981) pp. 396-399. I am indebted throughout this chapter to their excellent essay entitled "Religion and Social Stratification."

[8]Demerath, "Social Stratification and Church Involvement," p. 151.

[9]Russell Dynes, "Church-Sect Typology and Socio-Economic Status," *American Sociological Review* (October, 1955).

[10]Charles H. Cooley, *Social Organization: A Study of the Larger Mind* (New York: Charles Scribner's Sons, 1909), p. 23. Quoted in Rodney Stark and Charles Y. Glock, *American Piety: The Nature of Religious Commitment* (Berkeley: University of California Press, 1968), p. 163.

[11] Stark and Glock, *American Piety*, p. 165.
[12] Chalfant, *et al., Religion in Contemporary Society*, pp. 389-392.
[13] *Ibid.*
[14] *Ibid.*
[15] *Ibid.*
[16] *Ibid.*, p. 386.
[17] *Ibid.*, p. 387.
[18] John R. Earle, Dean D. Knudsen, and Donald W. Shriver, Jr., *Spindles and Spires: A Re-Study of Religion and Social Change in Gastonia* (Atlanta: John Knox Press, 1976) pp. 109-119.
[19] *Ibid.*, pp. 110-112.
[20] *Ibid.*, p. 114.
[21] *Ibid.*, p. 115.
[22] *Ibid.*
[23] *Ibid.*, pp. 116-118.
[24] *Ibid.*, p. 118.
[25] *Ibid.*
[26] *Ibid.*
[27] Carl S. Dudley, *Making the Small Church Effective* (Nashville: Abingdon Press, 1978), p. 35.
[28] *Ibid.*, p. 32.
[29] Lyle E. Schaller, *The Small Church Is Different* (Nashville: Abingdon Press, 1982), p. 27. See also pp. 28-41.
[30] *Ibid.*, pp. 28-41. See also Jackson W. Carroll, ed., *Small Churches Are Beautiful* (New York: Harper & Row, Publishers, Inc., 1977) and David R. Ray, *Small Churches Are the Right Size* (New York: Pilgrim Press, 1982).

Chapter 9

[1] Charles Y. Glock, Benjamin B. Ringer, and Earle R. Babbie, *To Comfort and to Challenge* (Berkeley: University of California Press, 1967), p. 93.
[2] *Ibid.*, p. 96.
[3] *Ibid.*, pp. 98, 104-107.
[4] Demerath, "Social Stratification and Church Involvement," p. 149.
[5] Stark, "The Economics of Piety," p. 495. Quoted in H. Paul Chalfant, Robert E. Beckley, and C. Eddie Palmer, *Religion in Contemporary Society* (Sherman Oaks, Calif.: Alfred Publishing Co., Inc., 1981), p. 396.
[6] Richard Sennett and Jonathan Cobb, *The Hidden Injuries of Class* (New York: Random House, Inc., 1973), p. 241.
[7] Nicholas J. Demerath, III, *Social Class in American Protestantism* (Chicago: Rand McNally & Co., 1965), p. 198.
[8] Charles Y. Glock and Rodney Stark, *Religion and Society in Tension* (Chicago: Rand McNally & Company, 1965), p. 8.
[9] Emile Durkheim, *The Elementary Forms of Religious Life*, trans. Joseph Ward Swain (New York: Collier Books, 1961), see esp. pp. 337-461. Cf. Randall Collins, *Conflict Sociology* (New York: Academic Press, Inc., 1975), p. 58.

Chapter 10

[1] Beth E. Vanfossen, *The Structure of Social Inequality* (Boston: Little, Brown & Co., 1979), pp. 246-279.

[2]William F. May, "Code, Covenant, Contract or Philanthropy," *Hastings Center Report*, 5 (Dec., 1975), pp. 31, 33.
[3]*Ibid.*, pp. 34-35.
[4]*Ibid.*, p. 33.
[5]*Ibid.*, p. 35.
[6]*Ibid.*, p. 31.
[7]Andrew M. Greeley, "Take Heart from the Heartland," *Overcoming Middle Class Rage*, ed. Murray Friedman (Philadelphia: The Westminster Press, 1971), pp. 331-343.Used by permission of *The New Republic* © 1970, The New Republic, Inc.
[8]*Ibid.*, p. 336.
[9]*Ibid.*
[10]*Ibid.*, p. 340.
[11]*Ibid.*, pp. 341-343.

Chapter 11

[1]Beth E. Vanfossen, *The Structure of Social Inequality* (Boston: Little, Brown & Co., 1979), p. 233. Copyright © 1979 by Beth Ensminger Vanfossen. Reprinted by permission of Little, Brown, and Company.
[2]*Ibid.*
[3]*Ibid.*, p. 235.
[4]*Ibid.*, p. 236.
[5]Mike Miller, "What Is an Organizer," *Christianity and Crisis* (April 13, 1981), p. 99.
[6]*Ibid.* I am indebted to Miller throughout this section.
[7]*Ibid.*, pp. 110-111.
[8]Janice E. Perlman, "Grassrooting the System," *Social Policy* (September–October, 1976), 7, 2, p. 405. Quoted in Fred Cox, *et al.*, eds., *Strategies of Community Organizations: A Book of Readings* (Itasca, Ill.: F. E. Peacock Publishers, Inc., 1979), p. 414. I am indebted to Perlman throughout this section.
[9]*Ibid.*
[10]*Ibid.*, p. 406.
[11]*Ibid.*
[12]*Ibid.*, pp. 406-407.
[13]Harry C. Boyte, *The Backyard Revolution: Understanding the New Citizen Movement* (Philadelphia: Temple University Press, 1980).
[14]*Ibid.*, p. 75.
[15]*Ibid.*
[16]*Ibid.*, p. 99.
[17]Joe Holland, *Flag, Faith and Family: Rooting the American Left in Everyday Symbols* (Chicago: New Patriot Alliance, 1979), p. 7. Quoted in Boyte, *The Backyard Revolution*, p. 23.
[18]Paul Levy, *Queen Village: The Eclipse of Community* (Philadelphia: Institute for the Study of Civic Values, 1978), p. 76. Quoted in Boyte, *The Backyard Revolution*, p. 23.
[19]Boyte, *The Backyard Revolution*, p. 19.
[20]*Ibid.*, p. 178.
[21]*Ibid.*, p. 179.
[22]*Ibid.*
[23]Richard Flacks, "Making History vs. Making Life—Dilemma of an Amer-

ican Left," *Working Papers for a New Society* (Summer, 1974), p. 60. Quoted in Boyte, *The Backyard Revolution*, p. 180.

²⁴"Bois d'Arc Patriots, Organizing in Dallas," *Green Mountain Quarterly* (Feb., 1977), pp. 9-24. Appears in Cox, *et al., Strategies of Community Organizations*, p. 436.

²⁵Daniel Yankelovich, *New Rules* (New York: Random House, Inc., 1981) p. 120.

²⁶*Ibid.*, p. 121.

²⁷*Ibid.*, p. 122.

²⁸*Ibid.*, pp. 244-264.

Chapter 12

¹Warren Haggstrom, "The Tactics of Organization Building," in Fred Cox, *et al.*, eds., *Strategies of Community Organization: A Book of Readings* (Itasca, Ill.: F. E. Peacock Publishers, Inc., 1979), p. 457.

²Albert J. Benavides, "The Catechumenate as Experienced in a Large Urban Mexican-American Parish" (mimeographed), p. 4. Used by permission of the Rev. Albert J. Benavides, Office of Parish Development, San Antonio, Texas.

³*Ibid.*, p. 5.

⁴*Ibid.*, p. 6.

⁵*Ibid.*

⁶*Ibid.*, p. 7.

⁷*Ibid.*

⁸*Ibid.* I would say that many blue-collar Protestants are converted but not instructed.

⁹*Ibid.*, p. 9.

¹⁰*Ibid.*, p. 10.

¹¹*Ibid.*, pp. 17-18.

¹²*Ibid.*, p. 18.

¹³*Ibid.*, p. 21.

¹⁴*Ibid.*, pp. 21-22.

¹⁵*Ibid.*, pp. 22-23.

¹⁶Harry C. Boyte, *The Backyard Revolution: Understanding the New Citizen Movement* (Philadelphia: Temple University Press, 1980), p. 192.

¹⁷*Ibid.*, p. 193.

¹⁸*Ibid.*

¹⁹*Ibid.*

²⁰Virginia McCourt, *Working-Class Women and Grassroots Politics* (Bloomington: Indiana University Press, 1977), p. 18.

²¹*Ibid.*, pp. 18-19.

²²*Ibid.*, p. 69.

²³*Ibid.*, p. 232.

²⁴Studs Terkel, *Working* (New York: Avon Publishers, 1975), p. 465.

²⁵*Ibid.*, p. 467.

²⁶Paul Tillich, *Love, Power and Justice* (New York: Oxford University Press, 1960), pp. 35-53.

Index

This index prepared by:
Karla Fredericksen
Mark Fredericksen